The Sacred Vessel

Mona Rolfe PhD

The Sacred Vessel

SUFFOLK
NEVILLE SPEARMAN

First published in Great Britain in 1978 by
Neville Spearman Limited,
The Priory Gate, Friars Street, Sudbury, Suffolk

Photoset by
Specialised Offset Services Ltd., Liverpool
Printed by Biddles Ltd., Guildford, Surrey
and bound by Mansells Ltd., Witham, Essex

Contents

Foreword

Much research has been done on the origin of the will in man. Theories have been evolved and many books published on the subject. And yet the nature of the will is still partly a mystery and is not wholly understood.

In order to understand how the will of man came into being we need to go back to the beginning of life and the early make up of man.

The will in man today, and sometimes even more in woman, is inordinately strong. How did it come to have the immense strength and why does it lead to either the finest creative work – or the most destructive and devastating happenings.

We need to understand that there are two wills, the will of the soul and the will of the personality.

In each life we come to earth to form a new personality under varying astrological signs. If during the life the will of the personality is brought under the guidance of the will of the soul – and the two wills become one – then the individual becomes dedicated to the work he has come to earth to do and the path is frequently clearly defined. However great the difficulties that have to be overcome, there is sufficient light to achieve the required result.

If, on the other hand, the personality decides to build its own path away from the guidance of the soul – then the individual may become lost and the life seem to lack meaning or purpose, and all forms of neuroses or psychosis may develop.

The great psychiatrist, Dr Carl Jung, said that of all the thousands of patients who had passed through his consulting room, not one who was deeply rooted in religion, or a philosophy was a lost soul – those who had no roots in a religion, or belief in a pattern of life frequently became neurotic and their lives were without foundation.

Before we come to earth, just before birth into the physical body, we see a blue print of the life we are coming to fulfil. After the death of the body, as soon as we arrive on the other side of life, we are shown a picture of what we have made of life. Much time is then given to a comparison of the two and an understanding of where things might have been improved and where something worth while has been achieved.

Man has been endowed by God with free will – and if the free will, directed by the will of the soul, creates a life in which he achieves happiness for others and enriches the lives of those with whom he has come in contact, then he knows all the joy of the artist who creates a great work of art, or the musician who composes great music.

We are on earth to use our free will to create, for we are the creative representatives of God, but unless the work achieved is under the guidance of the Divine plan, chaos may result. If we spoil the plan that we made before we came to earth in conjunction with others and so ruin their lives, then we create a karmic debt towards such souls.

If a soul has incurred karmic conditions in earlier lives, then he may come back to earth with the added burden of those conditions and already have a tendency towards a neurotic attitude and a negative view of life.

An understanding of the development of the will of the soul and the will of the personality leads towards the opening of that wonderful intuitive faculty, which gives the power to overcome so much.

The great test of life is the power to overcome. No man is

given more than he can bear, all is wisely adjusted to his capacity.

For there is no injustice in life – all that a man has in this day of time he has earned in the past and is the capital upon which he can draw today. He will be drawn to incarnate with parents who can give him the vehicle he will need for this life. If he is to be a musician, he will need an organism sensitive to sound and he may choose a difficult path of poverty and deprivation in order to receive such a body from his parents. But if he has rightly used his worldly possessions in the past, then they will gravitate towards him in this life for him to use again for the good of others.

Mona Rolfe came to earth to be born into an Irish family where the mystical gifts were her natural heritage. Her twin soul in the world of spirit, Oneferu, came close to the earth to give the teaching through her. This book was given in the form of lectures between the years 1952 and 1963. Much of the teaching goes back into the past to give an understanding of the beginning of life and how man gradually developed from almost a puppet to an independent individual with the power to take decisions for himself and yet to work under the guidance of God. It brings us to the present day of time, showing the path man has come to earth to follow from God and back again, having suffered and learnt much in the material world. Some of the writing is prophetic and shows man the path of the future and the meaning of the years to come.

The soul is a sacred gift from God and is the vessel which holds the mind which controls the will of man.

Betty Shephard

'In the heaven of Christ, the Christ-Force, the colours are white with mystic whiteness which comes with the glorious visions of the Christed ones, like drops of liquid diamonds upon a shimmering white background of light. All the colour which comes to the Christ plane emanates from the God plane, and the colour is ever moving downward, forward and round, so that the Christ plane can ever be filled with the power and the glory of God, and it is on this plane that those who were destined to come to earth as Christed ones dwelt. It was this Christ power that they learned to absorb and understand. It was this Christ power that they learned to give out when the time for their great journey to the planet earth came to its fulfilment.'

The Origin of Life

The origin of life is a vast subject – but we will try and reach a conception of God and Light aeons of time before the era of Creation. The glory of the Mind of God as He set in motion His mighty plan for the creation of man.

Endeavour to visualise a vast source of light, moving, glistening, strong, with many colours, radiating from a centre or a focal point towards the outer edge of light, a condition of light which it is almost impossible to describe in human terms. And in the very centre of this glory of light there is a symbol, and that symbol is one single eye.

The eye is open, the lashes long, the eyebrow is strongly marked, the colour both of the iris of the eye and of the surrounding of the eye is constantly changing, and it changes through the alternation of the rays used in projecting that eye through light, into light and beyond light.

As we look at it we believe that the eye is motionless, and yet, as soon as we begin to contemplate the glory and the radiance surrounding it, we are conscious of another symbol which appears behind it. We look, metaphorically speaking, through the eye beyond light, and beyond light we are conscious in light of the symbol of a heart, the Heart of God, for we are privileged to contemplate the House of God.

In the Bible when the Master Jesus says 'In my Father's House are many mansions', this is the House to which He refers and the mansions are the degrees of light encircling,

11

filling and enfolding the whole.

It is with that thought in your mind – 'In my Father's House are many mansions' – that we contemplate these symbols.

For in the centre is God, entirely alone, entirely whole, Holy, Created Being of Light, and we must remember that God never sleeps. Therefore as we contemplate the Mind of God symbolised by the eye, and the Heart of God symbolised by the heart, we are conscious of a Being of Glory and Light in whom there is no flaw, who sleeps not day, or night because to Him, day and night are altogether one in light.

We are still contemplating the symbol of the eye, and as we reach out it seems to be withdrawn into the background as if it was absorbed by the movement of light and colour which flowed over it and around it, and in place of the eye there appears another symbol, a symbol which is familiar to those who have studied ancient history, and particularly ancient Egyptian history, the Cross of Light, the Ankh.

The Ankh is not entirely like the Cross of the Crucifixion of Jesus. Where the Cross of the Crucifixion has a plain upright from the ground to the tip, the Ankh is made with a loop in place of the upright above the cross-beam, and this loop signifies the complete cohesion of the whole.

The light flows through the Ankh from below, is absorbed and given forth from the centre. From the centre it accepts the gift of light from man to God and pouring out that gift of light above, the gift is returned by God into the Cross again for the reincarnation of man.

The Mind of God projects Divine Thought, and as we see this Mind brooding and silent we are conscious of the great work going forward in created light from behind and within. We are conscious of an enormous outpouring of power which demands a purpose, which demands that this power and light shall not return to be absorbed in itself but shall go forth in the work of creation, and as the Mind of God creates, it creates man in the image of God. It decrees that man shall tread the earth within a physical body, arrayed in light from the

12

beginning, carrying light within his heart direct from the Heart of God, and through that light treading the path of earth in pure strength of light, a Son-Daughter of the Father-Mother God, the insuperable loop of the Ankh represented in the perfect twin-soul, one with God.

There would never have been any creation of man, nor would the divine purpose have ever been fulfilled through man, if the Father-Mother God had not accepted within His Mind the Crucifixion which was later symbolised and, in a sense, brought down to earth, by His Son-Daughter Arbal-Arbel.

For Arbal-Arbel came to earth in the body of Jesus, the carpenter's son, that He might bring the perfection of God into the life of man, that He might teach men about God, about the Place of Light, that they might create within their hearts such a desire for that Place of Light that they would model their lives on His teaching, which was the teaching He had learned in the Glory of the Light of God from His Father-Mother God.

Arbal-Arbel came to earth the perfect twin-soul and because at the moment of incarnation of the Master Jesus Arbal had not yet completed the work which linked Him with His previous incarnation on earth, an incarnation in which Arbal-Arbel the perfect twin-soul had been separated, Arbel, the female soul, volunteered to come to earth and to create the light of God in the body of Jesus.

The coming of Arbel was already light. Arbel had waited awhile in the hope that Arbal could complete His work in time to join Her but He was not ready, so Arbel came to earth, the feminine gentleness within the body of a man and undertook the condition of life which Arbal-Arbel together, the perfect Son-Daughter of the Father-Mother God, should undertake at the bidding of their Father. There were two occasions when Arbal joined Jesus and Arbal-Arbel became one: one, the moment of the Baptism in Jordan, after which Arbal was called upon to return to the Place of Light for further completion of His work in the world of spirit; and at the

13

moment when Jesus stumbled along the road to Calvary and Arbal replaced Arbel for the final terrible physical suffering.

We cannot study the history of Creation and the Book of Genesis in the Bible unless we link it, step by step, with the incarnation of Arbal-Arbel. At the moment when the Divine Mind of God, within the House of the Personified God, created man in His own image, He set going a circle of creation which must continue until man either finds regeneration through understanding and light, or damnation through the power of the darkness.

At the moment when the perfect Son-Daughter of God was first created a Being of Light, our Father-Mother God created also many Son-Daughters. The first we might call an older generation. These unnumbered numbers of Son-Daughters He created of Light from the Divine Overplus of the Creation of the first Son-Daughter. They were those who were called upon to be the leaders of created man throughout the whole life of man ordained by God.

Here we see the life of man ordained by God; that whole life span from the beginning when God set His seal upon the forehead of created man to the moment when, perfected through plane after plane of consciousness, finishing with the earth plane, man returns through plane after plane of consciousness to the House of His Father-Mother God.

The Ray Children

We come to the point where our Father-Mother prepared the precious drops of Himself for the creation of the Ray Children, the Children of the Breath.

These drops were of the Divine Overplus and they were used to people the seven planes of consciousness of which the seventh plane is Heaven, above which rests our Father-Mother God, our Father-Mother-Son God, engaged in the preparation of the Children of the Breath for their incarnation into matter aeons of time later.

The Ray Children are the Children of the Breath, the very Breath of God drawn from the heart of God, created in the image of God, to prepare the way of life for a new Christ.

These Ray Children are incarnate in the body and in the various degrees of etheric bodies within those seven planes of consciousness between earth and Heaven in vast numbers, carrying with them an immense light direct from the Father Himself and learning to use that light in the service of God to His Glory and Honour.

The Ray Children are created of light and sound and colour. They are sensitive to the Presence of the Father-Mother God. They are conscious of dwelling with Christ Jesus as they are conscious of the presence in their midst of Him whom we know as the Buddha, Krishna and all other Christs who have come under the aegis of other lands in other times.

The dominating colour with the Ray Children is amethyst

and that amethyst can from time to time be projected in the world of men in very large quantities. That ray will touch the power of the spirit in whatever soul it contacts and the force of that ray will draw the power, the light, the strength, the glory, from within that soul which is the very Heart of God.

Our Father-Mother God gave no other name to these Children of the Breath, the Ray Children. You may recognise them as you go through the world of men; you may not. The recognition is a linking up from heart to heart, a recognition of touch, a gentleness of sympathy and understanding and a friendship which neither oceans nor continents can break.

Some will have met in previous lives. They find the earthly-bodies difficult to hold. Many of them are engaged in unusually heavy work in the world of men, menial tasks which try the body sorely and vex the soul. Many are placed in the dark places of life where they must hold their light within themselves and use it at all times for the rejection of darkness.

But they are never alone; they are always conscious both of the Presence of the Master Jesus, Christ of the Piscean Age to which they approach most nearly, and of the Glory of God who is able to pass through them messages to those who are called sons on earth, messages which will strengthen and guide the many people in the world of men.

They are entirely without thought or consciousness of self. Their only desire is to use the power, that great gift of God, in the service of God and for the regeneration of mankind.

Some of them are being used as channels for the higher world of spirit. Many have even had to renounce that joy and to move among men carrying the praise of God in their hearts, obedience, humility, faith, prayer, meditation, and yet feeling nothing of the Glory of God, or of the light of His ways.

They do not come back with karmic debts to clear. Sometimes they will be called upon to cleanse and purify a plane of consciousness, or an ancient Temple which has incurred much karma against the Father-Mother God, but they themselves carry no burden of karma and therefore such sickness or disease as comes their way is part of the chosen path of life which they have accepted before incarnation.

They are nameless. They are under the guidance of the nameless one whose voice they hear, whose visage they see not. And the only ones to whom a name is given are those who dwell within the seventh Heaven and these our Father-Mother God has called the Sons of the Morning.

The Sons of the Morning are specially prepared channels. They dwell in the ethers of light; they are not within a physical body at all. They have never touched the astral plane, the astral darkness or the astral inhibitions. They are called upon to guide those other Children of the Breath who, working on the planes of consciousness between the seventh Heaven and the earth, must accept through them direct, the light of the presence of the Father-Mother God.

From time to time the Sons of the Morning are withdrawn into the place of God. They indraw the Holy Breath; they worship at the Mercy Seat; they kneel in humility before the Place of Light, God Omnipotent, God Holy, God All-wise. And those etheric bodies of light which hold such radiance that it sparkles and shines even in that place of light in which they dwell, hold themselves ever pure and ever holy that they may take direct from God His very own Father-Mother-Son light and pass it through undimmed, unlimited, to those other Ray Brothers who are working in the worlds between.

We have heard up to now very little of the Sons of the Morning, but the work of the Aquarian Christ is to teach all those who are ready, to transmute the physical body into light, and that transmutation will at all times take place in full consciousness of man and full daylight, so that at one moment the physical body will be there in the flesh, a living breathing man or woman, and the next moment it will be a thing of light, held, guided, transmuted by the Sons of the Morning.

The work of the Aquarian Christ is to transmute the physical body when the time comes for it to leave the earth plane into light, so that as it walks over the bridge those who remain on earth will see a being given more and more light until it becomes pure holy light the other side of the bridge.

17

Later, if all play their part, there will be no bridge at all. What is the preparation we must make? We, the children of Pisces, moving out of the Piscean Age into the Age of Aquarius, anxious and ready to play our part wherever God calls us to fulfil it, we shall remember the power of our thought, for when we touch these planes of light we touch a vibration of light which can create or destroy. There is no negative thought in the light of God. Therefore, must we ever think with positive strength and glory in our daily tasks, our daily speech and our daily travelling.

We are not called upon to 'turn the other cheek' as we were during the teaching of Christ Jesus. We are called upon to examine the hurt which is given us and see whether any negative thought or action of ours has caused the hurt which has returned to us, and if so, to cleanse and purify it with light that nothing negative may go forward in the path of the Aquarian Christ.

For the Sons of the Morning are ready as they have never been ready before to call for channels of their light.

The Creation of the Children of the Breath

Life is a mystery — it is the existence beyond, without, or outside the Will of God. Those who dwell in the glorious radiance of the Place of God are part of God with an absorption of light which man in the physical body does not, and cannot, touch.

When the Divine Overplus drop by drop was caught and held to produce a being in the image of God the Father it was detached from the Being of God; it was separated drop by drop from the radiance of God Himself.

Each one of those drops of the Overplus of Creation held within its light, power, colour, sound, being, and by itself was entirely apart from God and individual.

These drops were gathered together to form the Children of the Breath of God. Each drop formed a being created by God within God, but outside, for that being was a living soul, and though a part of God was also a thing alone, an individual, created life.

During the hours of sleep you journey in the Place of Light, and you can only journey in that Place of Light because your heart holds that thread, that cord, which links you to God Himself. You have many times seen small children who are not yet able to walk easily by themselves with a form of strap about their shoulders which is held by the parent or guardian.

That is exactly the image that you portray for those in the world of spirit. You have that silver cord, the end of which is held by God, through which God supplies you with the force which is necessary to function as His child in the physical body of earth.

So when you return from the Place of Light after a night of sleep, earth's morning wakes for you and the work of earth begins. What is the work of earth? It is that material work, that material task, by which you earn your bread, through which you must learn to build a sure foundation, for if you are troubled about the work of earth you walk unsteadily towards the night of sleep, and if you do not sleep you fail to link with God, and if you fail to link with God you cannot absorb into your being through the silver cord that power of light which must rest in your heart that His radiance may shine through your eyes and manifest itself through your whole being.

When you hold a child on reins you leave it to choose its path, and when God holds you and places within you the glory of Himself, He gives you freedom through the power of the will, but you can only have that freedom and use that freedom if you learn to accept your part in obedience to God.

So in your meditation when you set yourself aside from material needs and withdraw into the silence the only thing that matters is that you should submit your will to God and when you have done that, the whole of life is simple and plain.

The mind of God within man is light; the light of God within man is mind. It does not matter what the scientists say, mind is the God within, and only when you can use your brain in such a way that it is guided by your mind can you accept earth's work at its full value and know and realise why God has given you life.

He has given you life that you shall learn to see one aspect of Himself as no other person can and that aspect of Himself you see through using your mind in conjunction with His, and although you are free to go where you will and to travel in whatever direction you wish you are nevertheless only free when you can submit your will to His Will through the power of your own mind.

The power of God outside you is form, and when you look at all things in life with the eyes of the spirit you see the shape of God within them because you see the purpose which God has used in their creation. Nothing is accidental; nothing is wasted. You may think that a long hard day has brought you no fruit to your labour, no reward for your pains and although it may not show for many, many months after, you will realise that where that labour has touched your life through God, God has manifested Himself through your work in the world of men.

So through your life on earth you live with God, in God, by God and through Him, but most essentially *in* Him, and when He is with you all things are possible. Nothing is beside or apart from the plans which you make for your earthly work, but all plans must contain the outward consciousness of God which is form, shape, preparation, and all plans must contain the inner consciousness of God, which is mind.

After the creation of the Divine Mother aspect of God, our Father-Mother God prepared the way for the creation of the Son aspect of God. After this third aspect of God when all was finished, He created His beloved Son, El Daoud – Daoud means 'beloved' and El means 'the' – and He called him close to His side. He explained to him with all the glory of light which He gave him, the work which He called upon him to fulfil in His, God's, service.

That purpose was to continue the work of creation which God had begun over a long period of time. El Daoud had collected the Divine drops of the Overplus of light, of colour, and glory, and poured them out until they assumed at his bidding, through the bidding of the Father-Mother God, form and shape which brought into being the other etheric worlds, and when all worlds were created, all worlds were peopled with different strata of life, the greatest light givers being those in the plane next to the God-plane and the Father-Mother

21

God, and the lesser light givers being further away from the God-plane of the Father-Mother God.

These are the things of the spirit as our Father-Mother God ordained in the beginning, that man should have form in His image and that form should be endued with the blessed power and light of Himself through the mind of him whom He called 'Man'.

You find yourselves today standing on a threshold. You have learned from life a story but you have learned it the wrong way round, for you have learned the journey of man on earth and forgotten the journey of man through God to earth. Now you are on your way back; slowly and painfully you are accepting the troubled path of life, blessed by the love of God, holding within yourself that great creative force which He has given each one of you to use in His service in a different way from your fellow man.

Why must you obtain this knowledge with such difficulty when you would be so glad to use it? To how many would you carry this wonderful story and forget to ask yourself whether they were ready to accept it, whether they would pour ridicule on it, whether they would go away with crooked lips, smiling, and pour ridicule upon you. The fact that these things of the spirit are open to you means that you have been called to undertake some special work and that work is the full understanding of the cycle of life, from the drop of Divine Overplus as it left the Father's side to its complete formation in matter in the body of flesh, and from that complete formation the development through that form of the mind of man which gave him the power to link consciously with the glory of God. With that knowledge to plan your life in His service in purification of body and soul in preparation for the moment when you stand and face the bridge of death, that bridge of death which to so many is a black thunderous cloud through which they are afraid to venture, from which they turn their faces and prefer to go on suffering physical pain rather than place one foot upon that bridge.

But that bridge is a glory of light; the substance of which it is made is strong enough to hold you; it will not let you fall for you have prepared God's image in the form of man and you have prepared your soul through your own mind to meet the soul mind of God.

Divine Eden

In dwelling in thought on the beginning of life, visualise a great park called by our Father-Mother God Divine Eden. This park looks to our eyes bare and barren for there grows there but one kind of tree and one herbage, and it is vast, it is radiant, it is glorious, but it is not a park in the sense that we know a park today.

This place, Divine Eden, our Father-Mother God caused to be the workshop of El Daoud, the Beloved, and He gave to El Daoud the power to create living things; having Himself used the Word of Power of the Godhead for the creation of man He prepared a lesser word of power which He gave to El Daoud, the Beloved, and left him in charge of the creation of all animal life: animals, fishes, birds, beasts of all sorts and conditions.

The work of creation is caused by the swift movement of vibration, the swift vibration of light coming into contact with vibration of light or with vibration of gross matter, and according to whether the vibration is of light or of matter, so is the quality of the created, living thing.

Divine Eden was new in those days, new in the way St John the Divine uses the word 'new' when he writes of the revelations which were given to him upon the Isle of Patmos. The Garden of Divine Eden was washed and bathed in light and, therefore, the vibration was swift and sure and the creation within that Garden was beautiful.

The animals were harmonious towards one another. They were glorious and beautiful to look at, and the birds harmonious always, for these are the creatures of the Deva Kingdom, and in these is no darkness at all; and the reptiles and the fishes, still things of beauty and light, harmonious together in harmony and light.

Then did our Father-Mother God appoint as messenger, El-Daoud – Evam or Adam-Evam, the twin soul, to inhabit Divine Eden but to be sent first of all as the messenger of the Father-Mother God to the planet earth to watch the progress made by the created Beings of light created of the Father-Mother God Himself.

The word of power used by El Daoud, the Beloved, was bringing into being a most glorious animal kingdom. The word of power used by the Father-Mother God directing souls into gross matter varied very much according to the type of matter and the degree of grossness into which those souls were plunged, for the Father-Mother God created the Children of the Breath to whom were later given the name of the Dhuman, and the task of Adam-Evam was to direct the life of the children of the earth into the right channels so that they should be prepared, step by step, to be glorious temples of the very God Himself within their souls. And it was the task of Adam-Evam from time to time to bring back to the Garden of Divine Eden such of the Dhuman people as were ready and able to take that further teaching which should prepare them to fulfil the work of the Father-Mother God as leaders of mankind.

We must distinguish at all times between the word of power used by the Father-Mother God to create the living soul of light in His image and the word of power given by the Father-Mother God to El-Daoud, the Beloved, for the creation of the animal kingdom, but we are at the point now when we see El-Daoud-Evam incarnate in matter as Adam-Evam, appointed under the tree of the fruit of the apple, their own tree in Divine Paradise, as Viceroys – joint Viceroys of the earth, created in light to guide the children of men to become teachers and rulers under the wisdom of God.

There had already been builded and founded a glorious temple in Atlantis, and we now watch these created Beings being directed towards that Holy Mountain in which was no disharmony at all, but nothing but light and rejoicing.

We see those Dhuman who are ready directed towards that temple of learning where they were instructed by El Daoud, the Beloved, in the way of God on earth, and we see following them their own families and children who, while their parents were studying in the temple, were called upon to prepare the soil without the temple for growth to the Glory of God.

We see these children of the Dhuman race directing their steps towards El Daoud, the Beloved, who would place within their hands that drop of power with which they could touch the herbage, the trunk or the root of the tree and watch the transformation into something different, strange and beautiful. For the first time we watch the tree blossom and as that blossom was brought forth, insects were brought into being by El Daoud, the Beloved, to suck the nectar of the blossom, that nectar which was symbolic of the tree's gift to man in service to God, the nectar of sweetness, of harmony and love.

We see the younger Dhuman children engaged in preparing the soil, smoothing it and sifting it and preparing it to make it a place beautiful for their parents to behold when they emerged from their studies in the great temple. We see El Daoud, the Beloved, walking in the garden in the cool of the evening and reporting to the Father-Mother God that all was well, and he would glance at the children engaged close to the soil in preparing in their turn to make all things lovely in the sight of God. He would pass to them those precious drops of light which would cause the flower to grow in the soil and the grass to blossom and the rose to flourish.

You will see that those who thus tended the gardens and grew up in the gardens were not actually the Dhuman; they were the children and the children's children of the Dhuman people, for the Dhuman, created in the image of God to guide and direct the children of the earth, were held within the Temple of Light as priests, called upon to praise God for His great goodness day and night, called upon to shed forth the light which should increase the value of the rate of vibration of created light and which should prepare the life of their children and their children's children for all time that the souls within them might be of that unquenchable quality which the Father-Mother God looked for and called for from all who served. For as yet there was no mention of death, no realisation of death, but only light.

The Father-Mother God brought into being twelve Planets, and these twelve planets He caused to revolve round the earth in order to strengthen and increase the vibration of light, and from the rays of the great Angels – St Michael, St Raphael, St Gabriel, St Uriel and the others who served Him day and night beside His Throne, He caused a great power of vibration to come into force and from them were created our brethren of the Angels.

The Angels are of a different order of created being from the Dhuman or the Children of the Breath. Their work is different and they fulfil themselves morning, noon and at evening in praise and prayer. It is they who pour forth light which shines upon the great Planet of God behind the Sun that directs its light to Venus from the Angelic Beings of God our Brethren, the Angels.

The Angels are aloof and apart; they do not mingle with the Dhuman, for they rarely touch El Daoud, the Beloved, or his work in the Garden of Divine Eden, but their vibration and their light is necessary to every change which takes place, whether in the great temple of the priesthood in the great temple of learning, in the Garden of God, or in the humble, lowly place called earth, the great force projected by the Angelic Host created light and light and light again which is shown to you in the cleansing, purifying flame of Whitsuntide.

Creation of Life on Lemuria

At the time of the creation of the planet earth our Father-Mother God created also eleven other planets. None of these planets did He people except the earth, but He gave to one of His great Angels charge of a planet so that twelve angels had charge of the twelve planets. In the fullness of time, turn by turn, each one of those planets shall be peopled with created life and the angel who controls that planet shall be in charge of the radiation of light from that planet and the Godhead.

For the planet earth our Father-Mother God did appoint a Viceroy, His Son-Daughter Adam-Evam, Adam representing the masculine side of the twin-soul and Evam the feminine.

There came a time when Adam-Evam took control of the planet earth and there were two other continents only in being in full cooperation with the Godhead – that of Atlantis and of Lemuria, and the four planets which were in the charge of angels who were to control the radiations to those planets, became in time peopled with beings of light who wore the coat of skin and gave light to the Godhead and who received light from the Godhead. But of these four planets those beings who peopled them were not of the physical body. They did not communicate by word of mouth, nor did they partake of nourishment, except such nourishment as they could draw through light in the ether which surrounded them. In their movement they glided and therefore both in their movement and their functions of light they bore no resemblance at all to

29

the creation within the Garden and Temple of Atlantis, to the creation of animal life upon Lemuria, or to the creation of man upon earth.

The power of vibration was a very real thing in the life of Adam-Evam, so real that in their descent into the gross matter of earth, they were obliged to add the consonant 'd' to the name of Adam, which had formerly been Eam, and her name, Evam, remained unchanged.

The story of the descent of Adam-Evam into matter is beautifully told in symbol in your Book of Genesis. You have there the full creation of the physical body unfolding the soul which is the glory of the Godhead and you have the life in the Garden symbolic of living nature, the trees, the flowers, and all that peoples the earth to make it glorious in the sight of God.

To Lemuria our Father-Mother God directed His Son-Daughter Satanaku-Eranus, and Satanaku was desirous to fulfil the work of God Himself. His soul tuned in to the Godhead on a very different vibration from the humility of Adam-Evam, and Eranus, his twin-soul, beautiful and shining as the day, was as yet subservient to the will of Satanaku in that she, at his behest, approached the Father-Mother God through the Father King and asked that she might be given the Word of Power to bring beauty into the continent of Lemuria.

She could not hold rightly the Word of Power. She broke the Word of Power in its repetition to Satanaku and he, using it wrongfully, created out of the mud and the slime of this continent which he had been sent to cleanse and purify with the light of God, for the purpose of his own service, creatures which had no semblance at all to the beautiful animal kingdom or to the kingdom of the birds for which the Deva were responsible.

These creatures crouched and moved in the slime and filth of the continent until the Father King in great distress called for the Father-Mother God to assist in its purification. Much of the darkness from Lemuria in time spread to the earth and

Adam-Evam, perturbed and horrified at these gross creatures which appeared in their midst, called upon the Father-Mother God to appoint a judge who would separate the darkness from the light by judging what was right and what was wrong, and he, because of his nearness in light to the Godhead, would bring light for that judgment.

Our Father-Mother God appointed a great Angel, Settharne, not to be confused with Satanaku who later in the Bible is called Satan; Settharne, the ruler of the great planet which later became known as Saturn, for Settharne is spelt in your language S-e-t-t-h-a-r-n-e.

Settharne divided the light from the darkness and returned to his own place or planet, but his task under the guidance of the Father-Mother God has always been to test the children of earth in light by setting obstacles in their path to see whether they had within themselves that purity of light which the soul holds from God to withstand the darkness and to hold the light.

It was at this time when the judgment of Settharne became something of great importance in the life of the children of earth that our Father-Mother God called into His service for the planet earth the twelve wonderful stars each of which had been placed in the charge of an Angel of Light, so that through the great power of light which our Father-Mother God gave from the Godhead these great angels drew the light and passed it as a guiding beacon to the children of earth.

During this time the beings in the coat of skin peopling four of the planets of light which lay between the astral plane and the Godhead, moved and vibrated to the purity of the God light within them, taking it and receiving it in perfect harmony.

There came yet another moment when those twelve wonderful stars linked through Adam-Evam to the children of the earth were able to draw light from those four planets also and to direct that light as intellect to the children of the earth.

31

The Return of the Twin Soul

We see Adam-Evam growing old in years, tired – very tired; although there is not the heavy burden of the flesh that we carry today, there was nevertheless very gross matter enclosing those bright and glorious souls, and they were beginning to feel that this clogging of the physical body must come to an end soon. They did not want to undertake any further plans or work in the world of men. They had fulfilled the task given to them – their work on earth – and they were ready and anxious to cross the bridge, and for them, the crossing of that bridge meant a great joy.

It was an elevation of the spirit, a glorification of the soul, which came to them when the command came from the Father-Mother God that they should lay down the physical body and release the soul which, by the power of the spirit, should return to God.

Birth into the physical plane to take on the Cross of Shame, that is, the physical body, is to all Dhuman-Adamics imprisonment, but death is freedom for the soul; no longer hampered by the burden of the body and the routine of life in the flesh.

So we stand at a moment when we can contemplate the work completed as far as it could be completed by Adam-Evam. That great, glorious, magnificent Temple in the Heights of Atlantis, with its twelve kings standing ready and waiting at the door of their subsidiary temples. The great

33

gardens surrounding it had been reproduced in Atlantis on the earth in every detail, and its completion drew near. The servants and workmen were laying the last paving stones of the court around the Temple, the walk by the great river. The trees stood in all their beauty with the names attached to the trunk that men might see and know what soul had been responsible for the growth of every particular tree.

The gardeners were looking eagerly over the flower beds to make sure no weed had been left, the grass was cut smooth and green and was ready for the visit of the angelic host to whose word was left the moment to pronounce the release of Adam-Evam. In the valley at the foot of the great mountain the Yevahics were carrying forward the pro-creation to which they had been called in service. Children were being born as infants and nurtured and cared for, to be brought up to serve God, and in a distant valley the Golden Rose bush with green leaves, blossoms with golden tips, was ready to break into flower and to scatter its perfume on the ether.

Adam-Evam waited for one more command from the Father-Mother God. In the Place of Light during the period of their work on the earth plane there had been prepared great souls – initiates – who were called upon to inscribe upon the tablets the history of the Temple and the building thereof, the plan of its courts and the light thereof, and these initiates were also learned in the sacred language of symbol, colour and sound, for as yet no word such as you know it had been uttered; the only language used was used by initiates and it was the language of symbol, colour and sound – all these three attributes of development which you, on the backward turn of the cycle, are now spending yourselves to learn. You do not demand to speak to God with the word of man, but to hear His Voice in symbol, in colour and in sound.

The great activity of body which had been manifested by Adam-Evam became much slower; no longer they joyed in climbing the hill and descending into the valley; they sat on the white stone benches in the courtyard of the Temple and observed the work of God that it was good, and night and morning they prayed that the soul might be released from the burden of the body and that they might be free in perfect unity and twinship to return to God.

They had much to learn from each other, for all twin souls who are separate in the body learn different lessons of life, but when they come together again in the world of spirit those lessons belong to both, so that where twin souls are separate the learning is much greater, the suffering more intense, the work more prolonged. There comes a moment when they feel they can no longer be apart, that they must each give to the other the complete experience of his-her own life, and that is the great attribute of twin-souls, their God-given desire to give, to give of the experience which they have had, to spare the suffering which they have suffered and to return to God in double measure the joy which He had given.

After Adam-Evam had returned to God and a new Viceroy was appointed, the world became a much more material place and all the records of life on earth were kept within the precincts of the Temple. No man outside the Temple, no Yevahic, no one wearing the cross of shame, was ever permitted to use the tablets and what you would call a pencil now, for Satanaku had threatened, as soon as he realised the great Glory of God in the Creation of Earth, that he would sow his evil through the written word, therefore the written word was held sacred by the priest-initiates in the Temple and never allowed over the threshold, nor was anyone outside the Temple permitted to use the written word any more than he was permitted to use the Word of Power.

And how well Satanaku kept his promise. It is through the written word that his greatest evil is done, his written word penetrates the minds and brains of men and only the Dhuman-Adamics know of his power and know how to guard themselves against it.

When the moment comes for the change called death to come into operation, there is a great gathering in the world of spirit and from that gathering are chosen and commanded those souls who will best help the soul who is to be called over

35

the bridge. They are prepared for quite a long period of time, in order that they may pick up the threads of the life of the soul, and among them is always one, preferably a twin-soul, who has followed through his own earthly incarnation the life of the departing soul, someone who, from his great knowledge of earthly conditions and earthly joys and woes and earthly life, can so enter into the aura of the soul to be met on the other side of the bridge that that soul will feel no strangeness, no uneasiness, no fear.

For many days before the departure of the soul from the physical body, the soul is called during the hours of sleep to meet this group of people who know the soul; he will come back from sleep and say that he has dreamed of so-and-so, or he would describe perhaps a relative, someone he has met in sleep and feels he knows but cannot place.

And then the call goes forth, again this is the language of sound. The first symbol is given to him, then the sound is given to him, and then both symbol and sound are surrounded with colour. The colour will be his own particular coloured ray on which he has based his life on earth, the ray of his Doorkeeper and his Spiritual Guide, and if he is a great teacher or great philosopher then the ray of the great soul who guides him inspirationally in his work on earth.

The arrival on the other side of the bridge is of great simplicity. When the call has gone and the soul has answered it, he is ready to cross the bridge as soon as the silver cord is snapped, and how free he feels when that cord snaps. There is no sorrow in the heart of the Dhuman-Adamic when he feels that freedom and manifests in light, when he has been held down and hampered by the force of the physical body. With joy he runs across the bridge and meets and embraces those who wait for him. Everyone who waits for him holds the symbol, the colour and the sound which have been given to him during those hours of sleep so that he knows them by their etheric signs not by the spoken word.

They move swiftly and surely; there is no hesitation as they lead the way and he follows, and they take him to a place of

36

rest and refreshment where again there is light and colour and sound so that he is enwrapped in those three attributes of God which are especially his own.

When he is rested and refreshed and has drawn from the ether, light which he needs to sustain him for the rest of his journey, he is given what you would perhaps call a holiday, for he is set down in the great Garden and there he may do what he likes so long as he does not journey too far from those who have met him. Only when he himself feels he has had enough of the Garden and wishes to go further he is taken further for teaching, into the great Temple on the Heights.

He will have seen temples on the earth, great cathedrals and chapels which have moved him with the beauty of their architecture and their colour, but nothing that he has seen on earth can compare with this great Temple. The Architect who designed this Temple under the guidance of God is none other than him whom you know as Pythagoras, the great and very important Master-Initiate, again a Master of remarkable colour and sound, who moves noiselessly and commands when the Great Bell shall call the worshippers together.

For many days the soul will remain in the precincts of the Temple, going in and out as he wishes, wandering in the garden, sitting by the stream contemplating the flowers and the men at work among them. He will have no desire at the moment to go and search for his tree; he has already discovered his tree in the garden he has left and therefore for a moment or two he does not realise the vital importance of that tree. Only when he has learned more at the feet of the High-priest will he journey afar in the forest in search of it.

He is not yet ready for the white robe; that has to be earned. The cloth is being woven by the servants of the Sanctuary – those servants who have created such beauty of texture and colour and material in the great Temple of Light in their endless service and by their great desire to put forth for God their all.

It is in this Temple a little later on that the soul who has passed will meet his twin-soul and then he will realise that already in the garden of the seventh plane of the astral how different he or she looks. Then the great joy of recounting in symbolic language the experiences of earth. Perhaps they have not met at all during this last incarnation, the sharing of these experiences, the giving to each other, and the great joy of freedom.

It is not easy to come into life on earth as a Dhuman-Adamic. The obligations of such a soul are so much greater than the ordinary people. Great gifts of a spiritual nature are the lot of the Dhuman-Adamic and great suffering also, and that suffering is not always suffering of a physical nature but suffering of a mental nature because there is so much that they fail to understand.

The Search for the Rose of Light

The search for the Golden Rose in the valley in Atlantis was an important event and we have reached exactly that point again in this cycle of evolution. So we will touch the various incidents which led to the plucking of the Golden Rose and see how that moment links with us today.

Many of those who are engaged in growing roses at the moment are striving to make perfect a large single golden rose. Those who have private gardens and have the urge to purchase a new rose, would find it beneficial to look for this large single rose and to cultivate it even though there is very little resemblance to the exquisite Golden Rose of the Atlantean Valley.

If we take our memory back into the past and endeavour to obtain inspiration from the beginning of time and the founding of the great temples we shall find that we belonged, at one moment, to an immense etheric temple founded by the Father-Mother God, in which at morning and at eventide the Father desired that all who served around the Throne with Him should meet for praise and worship.

Within this Temple, all who served were clothed in etheric bodies of light. They were perfect twin-souls, indivisible and one, and therefore the descriptions which were given down the Ages gradually became misunderstood, and the priests and the high priests and the servants of the Temple were known as soulless, sexless beings with gigantic wings.

There were certain sections of the Cherubim, Seraphim, the Plenipotentiaries and the Powers, that had wings, but the majority of the servants of the Temple had no wings at all – they had an etheric emanation which came forth from the spinal column, rising vertically up the etheric spinal column and expanding to a wide radius of auric light around the etheric body, and within this auric light were the colours of the rays to which they belonged and on which they functioned.

Then there came a time when the Father-Mother God wished to produce man in a body of a denser texture than the body of ether, and He prepared for him a coat of skin, radiant and glorious in light, filled with His Grace and His Glory. So below the great Etheric Temple there came into being another Temple of Light in which the priests, and the assistant priests, and the servants wore a radiant coat of skin.

There came into the life of the Temple about this time, what you would call, a routine. Those who served the Temple were infinitely more affected by the rays from the planets and the signs of the Zodiac than you are today, the radiance of light passing through the etheric body into the coat of skin caused a perpetual generation of rays of power, and therefore had you been able, as you are builded in the physical body today, to enter that Temple and to look within it, your eyes would have been so blinded with the light that you would have seen nothing.

From that Temple of the Coat of Skin there went forth a great desire to manifest the Glory of God all round the Temple, and there came into being great gardens of glory, flowers of radiant light and perfume, and majestic trees, taking a long period of time before they manifested to the vision of the dwellers in the coat of skin.

Then there came war in Heaven, for Lucifer, the great Being of Light, fell, if one may use the expression, from Heaven. He left the radiant place of glory and sought to set up a planetary system of his own, and he carried a great force of light with him. The star in his forehead betokened his close kinship with the Father-Mother God, the swiftness of his movements betokened the relationship to the Angels, who moved with such swiftness, such sureness, in the Place of Light. But within him was the heart which could not bear to think that Beings were coming into creation whom the Father-Mother God might perhaps love more than his angels, and Lucifer was one of the great angels.

From the moment that Lucifer left the Temple, creation – as you call it – came into being very swiftly, and the Father-Mother God, using strength of light and wisdom, crystallized the etheric particles of light which composed the coat of skin until the coat of skin became flesh, and the body of flesh was brought into the Great Temple on the Tableland, built in the ether and crystallized into the material world, and standing as an example of the Glory of God, which God expected man to copy by the work of his hands.

The priests and master initiates and the servants of the Temple were still perfect twin-souls. There was no birth, such as you know it today, they came into being from light, the light becoming crystallized into flesh, and within this body of flesh, the radiant glory of the soul linked expressly with the light of the Father-Mother God Himself and prepared the way of light for the Great Temple.

This Great Temple of Atlantis was placed upon one of the most glorious spots that man has ever known and may never know again. It was upon a mighty hill, flat at the top so that it formed a Tableland, and from the Etheric Temple there came into being glorious plants and blossoms, so that the whole of the hill was radiant with blossom, and beyond the garden stretched the mighty forest, whose trees were made as the earthly link with the children in the Temple on the Heights.

From the top of the hill, from the Tableland itself, there stretched green paths, down which servants of the Temple and the Sanctuary seemed to have no desire to move. They bathed in the great lakes in the cool water, they wandered in the gardens, and many of you incarnate today tended those gardens and made them wonderful and lovely by the work of your hands. For gardening was man's first physical labour for God, and none questioned or asked whither the green paths down the hill led.

Then the Father-Mother God created the children of the valley, and here we find an entirely different form of creation, for the children of the valley were called upon to bear their children as individuals. They were not brought into being from light, and therefore their whole outlook was entirely different from the Temple on the Heights.

There was no barrier between the valley and the Temple except a high wall of etheric light, and although from time to time the children of the valley became trained to the spirit and learned to hold the power of light with such strength that they were able, when called upon by the High Priest from within the Temple, to levitate from the valley to the Temple, yet they remained a people apart, and from time to time the Father-Mother God Himself came down into the Great Temple to accept the homage and the worship and the adoration of the children of the Temple, and He would look out on those green paths and know that one day the High Priest himself would journey down those paths to the valley.

So was man called to bear the body of flesh, to suffer birth into matter that he might know the meaning of death and eternal life. When the call went forth, the great procession would go forth from the Temple; the procession would travel down the hill, moving through the etheric barriers without hindrance into the valley itself. The procession from the Temple would be veiled from all children of the valley save one only, who, having attained the vision of the spirit, would come forward to guide them in their search.

Around the valley and within the valley was a great forest, a forest of a much coarser growth, much more tumbled and enfolded than the great forest behind the Temple on the Tableland, but nevertheless a forest, a forest which the Master Initiates and the Priests from the Temple would find incredibly difficult to tread as they were not accustomed to the coarse vibration and the coarse texture of the forest growth.

42

Their duty was plain and, guided by this one man, they would go forth into the forest to search for the Rose of Light. The tree on which this rose would be found was low, fairly close to the ground, with shining green leaves open and ready to hold the dew and the light, and it is possible that they searched for long periods of time and became very weary in their journeying before they found the one tree which would bear the rose. Then, with the temple service on their lips and the hymn of praise dwelling around them in the ether, the Glory of the Temple on the Tableland and the Radiance of the Temple on the Heights, the sound would move through the valley, the deep note of gratitude expressed to God that this rose, which was the token of the fulfilment of God's work with and for man, had indeed been found.

It was a rose of exquisite shape and very pure in colour, the leaves practically transparent in the light and yet opaque in the shadow, golden, as its name betokens, and held close, the petals closed and formed to a point that the precious drops of dew which had fallen in the early morning upon it might remain held within the petals until the rose itself was laid upon the Altar of the High Priest.

Then we see the journey back from the depth of the forest in which the rose had been found to the foot of the mountain, and again we hear the strains of praise, music and melody, glory and honour and wisdom, going forth from the band who had gone out to find the rose, and if we watch we shall see the etheric wall part, the procession slowly move through it, and the wall close again. But it does not shut out the soul that has acted as a guide. He is ready and he is with them, and as they pass through the etheric wall their bodies become transformed into light. They move up through the power which you call levitation, until they reach the entrance of the Temple itself. Here, even before they divest themselves of the garments of earth, they will place the golden rose in the hands of the High Priest who will dedicate it to the Service of God for all time in the Glory of His Kingdom.

Each one who has returned at this day of time to prepare

43

the way for the Aquarian Christ, set out from the place of light with an etheric golden rose in his hand. You were not called to go down into the valley to search for it – you were given the symbol that you might carry it with you in your heart forever. Slowly you came down through one plane of consciousness after another, from radiance into lesser radiance, and lesser radiance, until the body of flesh enclosed you, and even as the children of the valley gave birth to soul, you became a soul incarnate into the body of a living crying child. The golden rose was in your heart and its imprint was in your hand, and it is through the power of the golden rose that the healing rays which come through the palm of your hand can manifest and be used.

You are at the turning point, to you is given the gift of the knowledge of spiritual things, the power to transmute the light of the spirit which is within your own heart into that great beam of light that none can or may dim, a light so radiant that not only will it transmute your own physical body into light but the physical bodies of others will also be helped by your work in that service.

So once again you stand at the foot of the great hill. The wall of ether rises before you. To each one, is given the word which will open the invisible way, and when the day comes and all is ready, you will move up the green path of the hillside, and the flowers will stretch all round you as far as the eye can see, and the perfume of those flowers will enfold you to strengthen you, for they are yours, for each one of you, in the beginning of time, planted your own flower in that garden, and you will be called upon to pluck it and carry it into the forest to your tree, that you may bear your share in the offering to the Temple when the physical body becomes transmuted into light.

From Pisces to the New Age

We think of ourselves as mediators rather than mediums, mediators between earth and heaven, between man and God.

As we move out of the Piscean vibration we become conscious of a certain change of attitude in ourselves, for the Piscean, that is to say, the man who is purely vibrating to the ether of Pisces, is a man of compassion, is easily stirred to sorrow, easily moved to emotion; all of which proves that the ether of which his etheric light is built is of a denser quality than the ether of Aquarian man, for Aquarian man arises through the Piscean ethers to the Aquarian ethers. This change comes to him from within, just the same as your own inner light radiates throughout your whole being, both the light and the higher consciousness, the personality and the soul, so this change of vibration radiates from within and you find suddenly that things of which you had been quite afraid before, hold no more fear for you and you are able to face your difficulties with the knowledge that it is something which lies before you, into which you must enquire and which you must conquer.

This is particularly evident to those who work with children and young people because the Piscean attitude of mind to the injured and the infirm, the decrepit and the aged, is always one of sorrow, of a desire to spare the being any anxiety or trouble or pain but the Aquarian attitude is quite different, for the child of Aquarius must learn to overcome, and to

45

overcome with such strength and courage that very few people around him realise how much he is overcoming as he goes about his daily life and his daily work. He will be moved to pity if he sees a cripple or someone in pain, as a natural part of the nature of spiritual man, but instead of groaning with such a one or for such a one, Aquarian man immediately asks within himself, how can I help that man to grow strong, for Aquarian man realises that every man, however much disabled mentally or physically, must take his place in the world of men, beside men who are strong physically and mentally and more gifted than he is, and so forth, and play his part beside them. That cannot be done if people around him are all the time pouring out emotion, sparing him difficulties or pain. No, the right way is to place power in his hand and teach him how to use it.

That is why you will find that the young people of today have very strong wills, because they need the determination to carve their way in life, and the strength of will, will appear more in some than in others, but in all must the will be strengthened so that the soul may find a determined background as a security for its life with the personality.

There are two ethers of which Aquarian man must be conscious as he develops. Consciousness of these ethers will come to him very slowly, and if it comes slowly it is all the better because it will be a stronger knowledge and a greater understanding.

Within Sanctuaries of prayer and meditation there is a vast sound ether, and the sound ether which you find outside these Sanctuaries is not a sound ether at all but a reflection of the true sound ether. That sound ether we can only achieve in all strength and understanding if we keep a place apart for our Sanctuary upon whose ether those who come to guide us can build, adding their contribution week by week, day by day, month by month, until the volume of sound ether in the Sanctuary is sufficient for every member of that group and the Sanctuary to partake of the sound ether itself.

The soul incarnate in the physical body, when it is in

habitation of the physical body, is not conscious of the sound ether. When you are outside the Sanctuary, the sound which you hear, the voice you hear from the world of spirit, the guidance you feel as a touch upon your cheek, are nothing but the reflection of the true sound ether. True sound ether is known to the seer as the harmony of the spheres, and it is the consciousness of that harmony that Aquarian spiritual man must learn to achieve.

When your body goes to sleep, your soul is removed to a higher consciousness, a plane of light, and most probably your soul is entirely conscious of the sound ether. It is conscious of the voice, the discarnate voice, the voice which is conscious of musical sound, which is entirely devoid of any earthly vibration, and it is conscious of the movement of ether, even as the swish of garments, as it moves through the various planes of consciousness towards the conscious plane on which it dwells during the hours of sleep. Therefore, the moment your body goes to sleep and your physical brain is stilled with the personality which belongs to it, your etheric consciousness comes into life as conscious of vision, and above all, it is conscious of sound.

When the soul is without a body, dwelling in its own spiritual consciousness during the hours of sleep, the astral body is part of the living cosmos of light; so that the astral body is merged with the Light and Glory of the Father-Mother God, of the Sun and the Moon, and other Planets, and of all the starry heavens. That is where the name 'astral' comes from. But it cannot occur, except in degrees of very high spiritual development, to man while he is in the material body.

When you are asleep you are functioning in the pure ether of sound, when you are awake you are functioning in the reflection of that ether only, and you will see, if you dwell in thought upon it, that if you go forward into sleep with dark and ugly thoughts, with anxieties and disturbances, that those will act as a barrier to your intake of light from the planetary system of stars, and therefore you will return in the morning unrefreshed because you have come back to the reflection of something which you have not heard during the hours of sleep.

Hearing is a state of consciousness, and when you dwell in the spirit you do not only hear with the ear, you hear with the reaction or vibration of every sense you possess. Therefore, your vision becomes hearing, because your clairvoyant vision is nothing but the realisation of the astral glory which is imparted to you when you touch the planetary system and become one with it. This sound ether is wrapped up also with the light ether.

We go back in thought to Atlantis, we wonder what the Atlanteans were like, how they differed from us, and in what way they passed down to us the great gifts of the mediatorship.

Those first Atlanteans dwelt in a consciousness which lay between sleeping and waking. They were at all times conscious of the sound ether which you touch during your sleep state, because they were part of the planetary system of light through the incredibly enlarged astral bodies of light which they possessed, but they were equally conscious of the coming into being of the earth forces, because it was not very long to them since the sun and the earth were one and the earth was broken away from the sun and parted from it at the moment when the great Temple on the Tableland came into being.

When you think of the Atlanteans you think of them as a mighty people, beings of radiant light, and when you consider the Master Initiates who functioned in Atlantis you realise that they were touching some form of light and radiance which you have not yet achieved, and that is the reason they dwelt the whole of their lives and time in a state which you do not know and will not know yet awhile, between sleep and waking, for they were conscious of the sound ether at all times which brought them light and the voice of God, not just hearing sound, or reflection of sound with the physical ear.

We are at the point in the return of that mighty cycle of

48

evolution when man shall again become part of the ether of sound, so that spiritual hearing and vision will be one with him, waking and sleeping. His body must be prepared to take those greater lights, his soul and his spirit must be prepared to leave the physical body more freely and more easily. That can only be done if man places his feet very firmly on the physical earth and is able to fulfil the physical task which God has given him with the whole strength of his physical being.

Do not reject the thoughts or feelings that you have from time to time when you are uncertain of the way to go or the way to act. Realise that in order to know how to tread the path of life you must dwell within the sound ether. The reflection of the sound ether is no good to you at all, you must be able to raise your consciousness so as to become enveloped with it, and to become part of that great solar system of light so that every star, every planet, every zodiacal sign, which is a group of stars, contributes its portion of light to your astral body and awakens it from within to sound and vision. For it is positive thought, positive action, complete acceptance of the Will of God that will open this world to you.

You will find that the most sympathetic planet towards you will be the planet which governs your own rising sign. You will find that the planet which will give you light on the astral plane in the solar system most reluctantly, will be the planet which governs the moment of your birth, not the moment when it is calculated as the rising sign, but the moment which is shown by the day and the month of your birth. That planet will, as a rule, put greater obstacles in your way of becoming part of the sound ether than will the planet which governs your true rising sign, for it is your sun sign, and there was a time when the earth was within the sun, was separated from the sun, and it is no longer a part of the sun, and is ever reaching out to attain the height of the sun, and the sun knows that his planetary work is to place the things of the spirit so high and make them so difficult of attaining that man will completely conquer his physical nature in reaching out through the ethers of light for their attainment.

Those who are interested in the soil and the plant life of the soil, and who like to feel the hands crumbling the soil, and hold the tenderness of the plants, will find that the sound ether will draw very near to them – it will be very close to them at such moments. You must therefore be careful, when you are at work in such a way, to be very harmonious within yourself, and if possible to fulfil your gardening duties with someone who is equally harmonious than with anyone who is inclined to hasten or overcome gardening difficulties an easy way. This will link you, of course, as all gardeners are linked, with the great gardens in Atlantis, for these gardens were the source of power which made it possible for the Atlanteans to descend from the Heights to the Tableland and from the Tableland to the Valley; in the same way, we must raise our consciousness from the Valley to the Tableland, and through the Tableland to the Heights.

The Power of the Spiritual Sun

We return in thought to the great Temple of Atlantis. We have
frequently considered the incredible quality of the light in that
Temple. When we think of it we call it the Temple of Light
but there is much more behind the description in the word
'light' than just the light as you see it today, for we must
remember that the great Atlantean Temple in the Heights was
entirely within the radiance and the light of the Father-
Mother God.

The Temple on the Tableland, on a lower level of
consciousness, was entirely within the light of the Spiritual
Sun, or the power behind the physical Sun, drawing its light
direct from the Father-Mother God, but no longer entirely of
the Father-Mother God, a light lessened and transmuted by
its distance from the Father-Mother God into something
which was less than the light of the Very God.

It does not mean that the Temple on the Tableland was
dark. It was radiant. There was no night, for the radiance of
the Spiritual Sun enfolded it. Therefore, Atlantean man
functioned entirely within the orbit of the spiritual Sun, that is
the spiritual power which lies behind the physical Sun.
Because of that, he functioned upon higher levels of
consciousness than spiritual man today and he could see the
whole purpose of God behind the physical manifestation of the
body of himself and his brothers.

So you will realise that Atlantean man was one, not only

51

with God, but with his brothers also, and although he functioned on a lower level of consciousness than the glory of the spirit which he had known in the Temple on the Heights he was nevertheless spiritual man in the very highest and best sense of the word.

It stands to reason that when the people of the valley were created they touched the light from a much lesser angle, and therefore, in a sense, the spiritual power behind the Sun which was held by Atlantean man was not held by the children of the valley. They merely drew their light from the physical Sun and it was without inner illumination.

In reality the loss of that inner illumination came into being at the same moment as man became born an infant. So long as Atlantean man could manifest his being in the full glory of the spiritual Sun he was able, by the power and love of the Father-Mother God to incarnate perfect twin-soul adult in the light. There was no growing up. There was no cutting and change of teeth. There was no change in the bloodstream, no crises such as the child must pass through in his various ages of physical development. All those things were entirely unknown to Atlantean man.

In the beginning, the Earth was separated from the Sun. The Earth was at one time part of the Sun, and to become physical it had to be separated from the Sun so that the spiritual light which lay behind the Sun did not enfold the Earth when it separated and became a new Planet.

In those days in the beginning the Earth was enfolded in a fire-fog in which strange creatures moved and they remained as the only people of the Earth until the fire-fog had completely subsided and the Earth cooled down, and by its own vibrations made for itself a place in the Solar system. All this of course by the command and direction of the Father-Mother God.

Then came out from the Earth the planet that you know as the Moon, which had no light of its own, but was dependent upon the rays of the physical Sun to create light upon and within it. It was part of the Earth and because it was part of the Earth the vibrations of the earth held it aloft in space and the link between Earth and Moon was a very strong one, and is today a very strong one, for it draws the waters, it governs the growth of the plant and the tree and it affects the nervous system of man by its strange negative light.

Therefore, the more man develops spiritually the more he reaches away from the influence of the Moon, but the in-between stage which is a negative vibration acts as a very powerful pull, drawing him back to the Earth to prevent him reaching the spiritual light which lies beyond and behind the Sun. When that is achieved the power of the Moon over man, through the soul, is at an end.

After the separation of the Moon from the Earth had been completed the Sun was commanded to direct two planets towards the Earth to strengthen the positive power which could be so easily accepted and transmuted into negative light by the Moon, and these two planets are Venus and Mercury.

So the Moon was ejected from the Earth forces, as it were, to stand on its own feet and become a separate being, and Venus and Mercury were ejected by the Sun to prevent the disposition of the Moon from injuring the being who was shortly to come into incarnation as physical man.

You will find as your development proceeds that you will become more and more conscious of the negative power of the Moon. For your help and guidance you must reach through the physical Sun to the spiritual light which lies behind it in order that you may draw sufficient spirit power to prevent the action of the Moon from causing an unbalance while you are in the material body. As you reach out to the spiritual Sun you raise your consciousness to that state of light in which dwelt the earliest Atlantean Masters when they were conscious entirely of the Godhead and of the spiritual plan and organisation of the whole of physical life.

As you raise your consciousness you become more aware of the purpose of physical life, for you are touching the spiritual force behind the Sun which opens these doors to you, but at the same moment, in withdrawing from the physical material vibration, you are laying yourself open to accept the negative forces of the Moon, and those forces you will counteract by drawing heavily upon the spiritual beauty of Venus and upon the flood of thought and mind-development which come through Mercury.

Venus causes you to cleanse and purify your physical body because she loves beauty, and the body must be cleansed and purified in order to be an acceptable offering to the Father-Mother God. Those who are working with deformed or ugly children will find that as you transmute the spiritual power which is given to you for their strengthening and up-lifting the features will become altered and beautified, the skin will alter in texture, the eyes will adjust themselves because you are calling towards your work the power of Venus which was necessary to man in the beginning of time when the Moon was ejected from the Earth that Venus might be ejected by the Sun.

In your spiritual development you may not stand still. You may not be content to remain one of those who are conscious of an after life and ready to accept only the return of those you love and the nearness of those you love. You must transmute that love which they bring you on the vibrations of intellect into that greater understanding which brings you close to wisdom through the development of Mercury. For Mercury was ejected by the power of the spiritual Sun that man might develop the mind, which is the organ of the soul, through the power of the physical brain, and you will always find that the more you develop spiritually the greater will be your thirst for knowledge, your desire to study, to qualify even according to the earthly standards that you may link yourself with Venus and Mercury in order to balance the negative power of the Moon.

The life ether and the sound ether are neither of them heard or felt by man in the body until he begins this process of development. The projection of light and colour, the complete silence, relaxation of the mind, the power of the breath – all these raise man's consciousness towards the awareness of the life and sound ethers, and there will come a moment in your development when you will find, probably, that vision, which has given you comfort and strength and happiness, will seem to be taken away from you, to recede from you, and it is at that moment that your higher consciousness is being tuned in to the life and sound ethers of the higher consciousness of the heavens.

Much which seems at the moment difficult and obscure will be made clear to you, and you will see how important balance in spiritual development is, because you cannot build a life of spiritual man unless you can see the spiritual plan surrounding the physical plan of material life.

At times, an artist may become aware of the dullness of the atmosphere of England, especially of London, and find it difficult to paint in London because of the dimness of the light. For as his own inner consciousness reaches out to the spiritual light behind the Sun he tries to portray in that light what he sees, but finds he is only able to touch the ordinary sunlight of life which as yet is not sufficiently transmuted into spiritual light for him to be able to reach through it.

You will find over and over again that you will be guided to carry light to people who feel they want a greater light and cannot express in words what they mean. For to you, who are children of the light, the light in your great city is not dimmed, although the physical Sun seems to hide his face, yet you reach through that dimness to the spiritual light which lies beyond and when you are able to do that evenly and smoothly and with complete and perfect balance, your feet firmly fixed upon your material foundation, you will find that the whole of life will be radiant, for both Venus and Mercury will be pouring out light upon you from the spiritual Sun from which they come.

Initiation

We need to understand what Initiation really is. It is purification, but purification of a very special kind. To us, when we are in the world of spirit, the soul is the whole being of man. When that soul is imprisoned in the human body he is attached to a personality. Soul and personality are two but soul-personality is one.

When you, a spiritual being, set apart to fulfil some spiritual work in the world of men under the guidance of God's laws, planned your return to earth in this day of time it was for you, and for those who guided you and are still guiding you, a very important event for when the soul has a spiritual message to give, that soul is not permitted to slip through the ethers from heaven to earth for incarnation. It is a very long preparation and a dwelling in each plane of consciousness on the part of the soul before it enters the human body.

While you were in the place of light you would be one of a group of workers attached to a Master-Initiate. The work of the Master-Initiate has one definite purpose; he may be a healer, he may be a teacher, he may be both teacher and healer, but one of those attributes will be the most important one. But because he is a Master-Initiate he has himself passed through every phase of the experiences which we call 'Initiation'. He knows how far a student may be helped and how far he must tread the path of initiation alone, and he knows just exactly how much power and light and what coloured rays will be necessary for the student's path.

You, too, as the soul coming into incarnation, have a part to play. You must prepare for that descent into matter. First of all, under the guidance of your Master-Initiate, your Doorkeeper and your Spiritual Guide will be chosen. Although your Doorkeeper and your Spiritual Guide will be indicated by you, it is the Master-Initiate who advises you, and there is no choice.

You will spend a portion of each of your periods, which are equivalent to your day and night on earth in the company of your Doorkeeper. You will spend a similar period with your Spiritual Guide. Those periods will be spent in preparing for the great event of birth and living in the physical body. There will be a great deal to be done. You will have to meet those Great Beings of the Hierarchy who guide that particular group of Master-Initiates, and step by step, with all the joy and the glory of the light of the place of light, you will be guided by your Master-Initiate in all you say and think, 'say' being merely a projection of sound upon the ether, not the spoken word.

You will plan your life under the guidance of the Master-Initiate. It will be his advice that will set the plan of your Zodiacal signs and of course the planets which guide you under those signs, and there will be a helper set apart who will collect your past experiences. These will be studied and arranged in such a way that certain of them will be taken again, so that it will be a very long preparation. Your soul will be purified during the whole time of the preparation. The rays of light will be poured into you and then there will come that immensely important moment when the Spirit of the Father-Mother God will be poured into you by the Father Himself, that is His gift to you as you set forth, and that spirit contains a portion of the Glory of God which you carried to earth with you even though you may not remember it.

You will greet your Master-Initiate at regular periods of very short intervals in between. You will come to know him and to love him and to realise that his gentleness contains the power of the love of God and that his severity must always be with you and that you must understand the need for that severity if you falter on the path.

So you make that preparation for that immense journey to earth. The soul sets forth, descending, Oh so slowly, through plane after plane of consciousness until the moment comes for it to enter the physical body and be born a tiny crying child. It will probably be a long time before the Master-Initiate himself, to whom you belong and who belongs to you, will be able to manifest to your vision or your understanding, but he will be very near you through your life, and those whom you call your Guides will come under his instructions until the moment comes for him to manifest to you, and after that moment you will spend two periods in every twenty-four hours with him.

For a long time you will not even be conscious of his presence. You certainly will not be conscious of it during the waking hours of your day, but you may begin to be conscious during the hours of sleep and when you meet him pass it off as a dream. But all the time he will be guiding you towards those great steps of initiation which you have come to earth to take and you are not taking that initiation alone for yourself; you are taking it with a large company of men and women who serve and love the same Master-Initiate as you do and whom you will meet in your waking life without recognizing them, and during the hours of sleep with still less recognition.

We speak of a great spiritual Being named Gautama as the Buddha, and I wonder if you realise exactly what Buddha means. Buddha is an immense force of light, the greatest force of light in the world, because it is a combination of Christ rays enclosing within them the rays of the Cosmos and the rays of the Hierarchy. Therefore, when we speak of the Master-Initiate Gautama coming to earth as the Buddha, we mean that his great being, his physical body even, was able by its immense purification and preparation to hold the full force of this immense power of light.

59

Gautama did not come to earth only for that period in which he lived. He came to prepare for a new Christ whom he knew would be much greater than the Christ who would follow him and who would also hold the full force of the power of light that he held, plus certain additional rays of light set aside for the purpose, and it is this Being, prepared for 5,000 years ago, that we are expecting at the moment. We do not expect Him to manifest tomorrow. His coming is a very, very slow process. Everything that is touched by His power must first be purified and prepared just as you were prepared for your descent into matter.

Above all, the disciples must be prepared, and that preparation is by purification. That is exactly what initiation is. It is a purification of the whole being of man in preparation for his fulfilment of an immense work for God.

In the very ancient days this immense force of light could only be touched through the Mysteries and therefore Master-Initiates chose certain members of their people under the guidance of Beings of Light who set the pattern for that School of Mysteries in which they worked, and these, men and women alike, were set apart.

They purified their bodies daily with cold water. The purification of their garments was something of immense importance. Their food was fresh and clean and pure, untouched by the hand of ordinary people, and these people lived apart from the multitude, apart from the Court, apart from the world, and they studied in the silence of the Temple the great Mysteries. Through these Mysteries there were set for them certain tests which were tests for the Initiation and there were seven great trials or tests for everyone.

When the power was withdrawn from the Mystery Schools, so that man could no longer purify himself and prepare himself through initiation in the Temple, a great loss was felt, and this loss or blankness, this emptiness came to the hearts of men just before the coming of the Master Jesus, and that period would have been, roughly, about 3,000 years ago, so that during a period of 2,000 years, the chosen ones who were able to study the Mysteries were able to reach that tremendous Buddhic force when they had become initiates.

It was during this period that man, lost and alone, began to practise evil in the Temples, and it was during this period that the blood sacrifices were prominent among men, and then gradually the force of the incoming Master-Initiate was felt and the Christ ray was poured through the planet you know as the Sun, so that long before Jesus dwelt among men that Christ force was felt by man through the power of the physical Sun.

From the moment that Jesus was born, incarnate man was able to contact the Christ force direct, that was the great gift which the Master Jesus brought to man, and those among the rulers of the people in Rome and in Jerusalem who knew and realised what was happening sought to destroy Jesus because they did not feel they wanted the whole earth to feel the force of that ray or to become regenerate by it. They crucified Him, but in crucifying Him they released a still greater force of light which returned to the earth through the blood which fell upon the ground and through the etherisation of the blood, the first manifestation of the Christ of Aquarius was felt among men.

It probably will be a long time before the Aquarian Christ comes fully into His own, but all those who are set aside to work through their initiation under their own Master-Initiate, their Teacher, will move step by step towards Him and the purification which is necessary for the initiate will be carried out on all planes.

If your soul had come to earth to enter the physical body swiftly and without preparation it would have had no inner light which could expand and draw light from each plane as it descended. It would have had only grey ugliness which would have made contact with any part of ugliness in any of those planes and gathered it together, so that when the soul came into incarnation it would be a hideous being, lacking in spiritual light, with no knowledge of the laws of God.

In a sense your preparation for initiation is just that period reversed. You are on earth. Your soul is guiding your

61

personality through certain experiences on earth in order that you may become purified, body, soul and spirit, sufficiently so that the Buddhic force may touch you and hold you for all time, and that means that when you return to the world of spirit you will be already filled with light and you will make your contribution to the place of light as an initiate of whichever Master you are called upon to serve.

All countries, all peoples, have different forms of initiation, and therefore the souls that understand the value of these tests and trials will return to earth again and again and again, always seeking different nations, different peoples, for their incarnational period that they may learn through every possible angle and every possible point of view all that there is to learn about the purification of the body and the soul for the coming of the light.

You are the children who are leaving the Piscean Age behind you. You are held by the light which Christ Jesus gave to mankind. He did not mind if He never touched it Himself again so long as the people of the earth whom He loved should have the full power and value of it, and in order to test you He withdraws the light very slowly away from you during that period from Christmas to Midsummer and then He begins to pour it out upon you again until your whole being is filled with the Christ force in preparation for the Buddhic force which comes later.

The Brain

The brain is divided into four parts. At the moment we will deal with two of those parts, the upper brain, which is known as the cerebrum, and the lower brain, which is known as the cerebellum. With the upper brain, the cerebrum, you think and reason and take decisions; with the lower brain, the cerebellum, you register emotion, you control movement, and you control also the working of the whole body.

Your body, which is made up of blood and bone and muscle and sinew, of glands and nerves, and many, many organs, is all kept in perfect control and harmony through the lower part of the brain, which is called the cerebellum. Therefore, the lower brain has a very important work to do, and you will realise how over-anxiety, over-strain, overwork, can influence the cerebellum, or lower brain, and prevent the harmonious functioning of any part of your material body.

You are living at the moment in an age of mind, and because a much greater force and strength must be given to the upper brain, the cerebrum, by the lower brain, the cerebellum, a much greater attention must be paid to the perfect function of the cerebellum, the lower brain, otherwise the whole body will be out of harmony.

It is possible that you think of eating as a process in which you put food into your mouth, your teeth masticate the food, your palate savours the flavour, and your throat swallows the food, and you think no more about it – but there is a great deal more of importance to notice in connection with food and appetite than that.

Shall we suppose that there comes a moment when you feel hungry. That feeling of hunger is not just a message sent from an empty stomach to the brain; it means that all the cells and all the organs, the bloodstream, and the glandular system, are calling out for nourishment and saying that their work has come almost to a standstill because there is no digestive process in being. The feeling of hunger, which is an emotion, is registered by the cerebellum, or the lower brain, but before the cerebellum can do anything about it, it must communicate with the higher brain, the cerebrum, and get its orders from that controlling part of your mechanism; only when the lower brain has telegraphed the message of hunger to the higher brain, and the higher brain has telegraphed the message of hunger to the lower brain, can the need be satisfied and the body be set in working order again.

It is very important that we should understand these processes, because if the working of the cerebellum, the lower brain, is slow in a certain person, the message will be telegraphed to the higher brain slowly also, and the message will be received back again slowly in order to keep in perfect rhythm; the bodily mechanism will also be slowed down, and therefore you will find that such a person will be much slower to digest his food and also, strangely enough, far more frequently hungry.

If you have a clock and you wind it up, it rotates in a certain measure in a regular time which is signified to you by a tick-tock, and the same thing happens with your body. The rhythm which you know of in the spinal cord, which sets the rhythm of the whole of your body, is like the tick-tock of the little clock, and that tick-tock is communicated through the lower brain to the upper brain, and from the upper brain back to the lower brain again.

The organ, for it is an organ, which really holds the key to both the functioning of the lower and the upper brain, is known as the medulla. Some writers, and many medical men, call it the medulla oblongata to distinguish it from another medulla of a somewhat different nature, and through the medulla every nerve in your body passes. If you realise the number of nerves you have functioning in your body you will realise what a tremendous control of your physical and mental self the medulla has, because through it passes out every single nerve in your body.

The medulla, which in a sense controls the nervous system of your body, is an extremely sensitive organ. It is, indeed, the most sensitive organ which you possess, and it stands to reason that if your digestive processes are irregular or unsatisfactory, the body will be out of harmony and pressure will result upon the nerves, and this pressure will be communicated through to the nervous system through the medulla. Thus you find that numerous cases of neuralgia, many of the rheumatic conditions, and very many of the nervous tensions, the tics, or fidgets, or St Vitus Dance, have their origin in the condition of the nervous system which finds its way through the medulla.

It is important to fix regular mealtimes so that your body can use its digestive process at regular periods, and the digestive process is going from the beginning to the end steadily forward without interruption by absorbing quantities of foods between meals. It is important to keep your main mealtimes regular otherwise you will find your nervous system will be affected, and because the medulla, in the position that it is between the upper and lower brain, is such a vital point in connection with the brain, your brain processes will, of necessity, be slowed down.

Those who are accustomed to study are perhaps in the habit of taking some form of drink, coffee, or even fermented liquor, to keep them awake and to make them study. This is extemely injurious to the nervous system because the medulla becomes excited, and through that excitement it communicates a broken rhythm to the lower brain and a still more broken rhythm to the upper brain, and the little ease and refreshment you have had from partaking of this liquid

65

food is completely cancelled out by the violent reaction which will follow such partaking. It is wiser to take a larger meal in the morning and a larger meal before you go to bed at night, and to allow your midday meal and your teatime to be very plain and very simple indeed. In this way you will keep the body in a routine, working evenly and smoothly, and both your cerebrum and your cerebellum will be in harmony because the cerebellum will be able to send its messages forward to the cerebrum at regular intervals, and the cerebrum will know when it has to accept them and send them back.

In the centre, between the upper brain, the cerebrum, and the lower brain, the cerebellum, there lies an extremely important centre for the developing student – it is called the corpus collosum. It is also known as the spirit neuclion, and through that spirit neuclion passes the whole power of the consciousness. It is the centre of truth. The truth, the power, the wisdom, the Love of God, and the light of the great universe beyond your vision comes through the spirit neuclion and is held in the upper brain and used, when necessary, through the lower brain for feeling and emotion, for appreciation and worship, and for that great inner desire of the heart which brings man to serve God.

This spirit neuclion is in reality the thousand petalled lotus of Eastern religious teaching, and it holds the power over spiritual man because it is the communicating link with God. It lies close enough to the medulla to be affected, well or ill, by the condition of the nervous system of the student; it lies close enough to the upper brain to influence the student's power of reasoning, thinking, making decisions, and it lies close enough to the lower brain to control the movements of the body as well as to cleanse and purify from the body all that is unwise or which can take away the light from the etheric body of man.

When you are in contact with a medium, you will find that he has two ways of using his mediumship. Some will use entirely one way, others will use entirely another, others will use a little of both, but you may be perfectly certain, if you find a medium and a healer picking up your sensations either through the handling of an article or touching your hand, knowing where your pain is, and being overcome by those sensations, that he is a medium who is functioning almost entirely on the lower brain, or cerebellum, and such a one will draw most of his power from the higher regions of the astral plane. He will make a very easy contact with people who have recently passed over, and with every contact he will draw into himself, because he is drawing the systems, the sensations, the feeling, the emotions, of people and things into himself. He will draw in a certain amount of the vibration of the person, which he will not easily have the power to expel, and therefore such a one should always be given considerable time for the cleansing of their aura, both before and after treating or diagnosing a patient, because the condition of the patient's life will cling round them in such a way that they become the patient they are taking on.

The medium who is given mind impressions, mind pictures and symbols, is drawing inspiration through the spirit neuclion within the brain, and power from the plane of consciousness which he can reach when he goes forth during the hours of sleep. That plane of consciousness is a high plane, it is a plane to which he belongs, for he has been given permission during his earth life to raise his consciousness to that plane, and the power is drawn with clarity and strength in a straight shaft of light through the upper brain, where it influences his thinking and his reasoning powers and helps him to take decisions.

This form of development is slower, very much slower, than the method which links with the lower brain and gives the medium the sensations, but it is worth while, because the power which you indraw is pure, it is of God, and although at times when you have been emotionally disturbed or when, perhaps, through a long wait in the cold your body has become chilled, or through the wrong food your digestive process has been upset, you will feel all these things through the lower brain, and your thinking and reasoning and taking

67

of decisions will be slower because of the inhibition. It is nevertheless worth while to endeavour, through your development, to shut out anything which touches the feeling side of the lower brain, and to go direct through the higher brain, through the spirit neuclion which brings you to the power of God. But remember that that power must pass through your lower brain even if it later comes to rest in the higher brain and the spirit neuclion, for it is the lower brain which decides whether the right message shall be given to the higher brain in asking the higher brain for permission to function.

When a medium is in trance, the medulla, through which passes the nervous system, undergoes a form of paralysis. It is, in a sense, put out of action in order that the nervous tension, or the emotion of the student, should not influence the nervous system in such a way that the control is unable to come through and take complete control.

In the lower forms of trance where the medium is taken in trance by a relative of a sitter, or someone who has recently passed over, the upper brain, or cerebrum, will also be, in a sense, paralysed. If any part of your physical body is put out of action, the flow of the blood is altered, and this happens considerably under such trance conditions. Through the medulla and the upper brain being temporarily paralysed, the flow of the blood is impeded and it takes a little while after a trance condition for the blood to resume its normal flow. If this happens often – it is particularly the case with physical mediumship – the tiny globules settle in the bloodstream, which coagulate and become larger until they form a condition which is known to Doctors as Thrombosis. That is one of the principal causes of Strokes and Cerebral Haemorrhage, and so forth, in mediums of such calibre, especially those who are using their powers for physical manifestation or for healing manifestations through which sudden miracles are performed or demanded.

In a control condition the whole body, including the upper and the lower brain, is kept in perfect harmony of movement, the blood flows no faster, no more slowly, the nervous system is completely alive and alight so that the medulla shines within the brain of the student as a jewel, and the spirit neuclion is seen to us almost as a jewel, or chalice, for it is a chalice of light which radiates light from around it in the same way as those of you can see the picture of the Holy Grail when it is shown from the spirit world surrounded with light.

The Holy Grail is the material symbol of the spirit neuclion, and the object of the search of every child of God who comes to earth to serve God, is to seek the Holy Grail. He may go out as a knight to seek it in the world of men, but most of us are called to seek it within ourselves, and if we would seek it, we must remember that the body which God has created is entirely perfect in rhythm, and sound, and motion, and function, and that when we are developing our mediumship it must be such a natural process that the Grail itself within us is lit by the radiance from within our hearts.

The Grail, the Holy Grail within each one of you, is dependent upon the absolutely perfect function of your physical body, of the use that you make of the lower brain, which shows your emotions, your feelings, your appreciation, your gratitude, your humility, and of the upper brain which gives you your thinking and reasoning, and your ability to make decisions, but unless the light of God rests within the spirit neuclion, then that neuclion can never become the Holy Grail which you seek.

Some of you find your development in a Sanctuary, some of you must go forth and tread places which King Arthur trod to find where that Grail rests, and if there are some of you who have friends, or relatives, who cannot begin to take an interest in these things which move you so deeply, encourage them to read and study the Arthurian Legend, to visit the places where Arthur lived with his Knights and died, and gradually the power of the place will enfold them and their development will open out from within until they join you in the search for the Grail. No force must be used, you must never try and force your fellow student to the way of belief which you have, he

69

must come to it through the way that God has ordained for him to come, through the perfect function of mind and body in the Service of God, while your feet are set upon a firm foundation, a foundation which brings you, children of the earth, into the very heart of the earth itself, and brings you in touch with those men and women whom our Father-Mother God sent you out to know.

Divine Mind

If we go back into the past to the time when the first men as we know them walked the earth, we find man a very lonely creature. He understands very little of the world in which he lives and he seeks for something outside himself of which he can make an ideal and so he sets up for himself an image of himself which he makes of wood or stone or clay, and he talks to it and so on until he begins to feel it is an incident which is responsible for the good and evil in his life.

The Sun will be also such a god because his life depends upon the giving and the withholding of light and warmth, and the Moon and the stars hold the same place, and so we find individual man creating God in his image in order that God may be responsible for his needs and wants, his desires, his joys, his pleasures.

Then we go a step further. Man has now become many men and goes forth with a band of his own people to conquer another group of people who seem to have more of the world's goods than he has, and when he has conquered them he says to them – 'This is my god,' showing them his image of wood or clay or stone; 'you must worship it or worship him because he is the source of my life and your life, my power and your power.'

So we find he is forcing upon a tribe of people an image of God which he himself has created. We call that aspect of God anthropomorphical and we are moving away from that anthropomorphical vision of God to an understanding of a

Universal Consciousness, a power unseen yet felt, which directs the life of man and permeates it within the full force and glory of its being.

When you left the side of the Father-Mother God to come to earth you did not cut yourself off from that source of power and light; you brought it with you in such measure as your soul could hold it and it represented to you the basic force of your being. It represented the Will of God manifested through your soul in the physical body.

The Master Jesus came to earth at a very critical period in the history of the world. He came to bring an invisible force of light. That light had to be strong enough to penetrate the darkness of men's hearts at that period and to fill them with its power, which was the power of Divine Mind.

It is very difficult for you to visualise the state of the world when the Master Jesus came to earth. It was a world of license and wickedness, of ugliness and cruelty, far greater than the ugliness and the cruelty which you are facing today in the world of men. The Master, therefore, brought the love of God, which is indeed the power of Divine Mind, in a very, very large measure, and that measure had to be the full, positive complement of the negative darkness which enveloped the earth.

Therefore, His love manifested among men showed a very great measure of pity and compassion, and pity and compassion are the significant notes of the love of the Master Jesus manifest in matter.

Jesus came to prepare the way for a new Christ, and when the compassion and the pity which He brought, whose gospel He taught during His life on earth, had been accepted by the children of men it was transmuted into a different form of light which gave man a desire for an unfoldment of mental and metaphysical knowledge. Therefore, it is to be seen that before the Christ of Aquarius can manifest in the world, Divine Mind must be placed in the minds of men upon a mental and metaphysical plane. Only on that plane can it manifest as

Divine Consciousness and hold the hearts of men with its power.

This Divine Consciousness which is your gift, your birthright from God, has been trained by God ever since you were born. It was guided and trained first of all by your parents acting as a channel for the power of God under the Divine Mind or Divine Consciousness. Perhaps they did not sow seeds within your conscious mind of spiritual knowledge; perhaps even much of their way of living was an offence to you and an annoyance, even more so as you grew up. But you were in the right place as a child of those parents and whatever obstacles were set in your way, whatever uglinesses were placed before you to reject, whatever beauty was given you of mind and culture, it was for your soul, which is the mirror of the consciousness of God, to reject or reflect those incidents.

Were you strong enough? Did the battle overwhelm you? Were you unable to hold your own in childhood and adolescence? Or did you, through all the difficulties which you touched, still continue to manifest that light within, which showed God that you were worthy of a greater light? Divine Mind manifests through the material things of life. They were not given to you to make life worth while for you, but in order that you may show your Father-Mother God by the power of His love within you what use you can put those material gifts to. If you shut your heart against them, if you take the power and the interest which they bring for yourself, you are creating a negative band around your aura through which Divine Mind cannot penetrate, and therefore no matter what you do with the material gifts at your disposal you will find that they will not bring you that greater power of spirit which should be your right to have if you have used them wisely.

Some of you are set in places of responsibility and you realise as you look back over the years that mentally and metaphysically you have grown extraordinarily since you held that responsibility. Does that not prove that those material gifts which you have handled, you have handled rightly, for

73

they have brought back to you that greater power, that greater light, that greater colour which has given you spiritual strength to accept more responsibility and greater works?

There are two forces in the life of man. One is positive, the other is negative. When you work upon a positive vibration you are in tune with Divine Mind. You may be working in a coal mine; you may be working in a factory where you hear foul words and are surrounded with ugly thoughts, but you will have the opportunity of using the power of Divine Mind which has been given to you as a positive gift to God, and as that gift is positive, should you pour it forth upon the ether it is returned to you by the Divine Consciousness of Spirit in double, treble, quadruple measure from your giving.

If, on the other hand, your thought is negative, you have nothing to project, for negative thought is dark and heavy. Perhaps you are a grumbler; then you are creating around yourself a world of negative thought which the positive light and love of God cannot pierce or penetrate. Perhaps you are someone who likes to be ill and rather enjoys being fussed and cossetted and pitied. You are shutting the whole of that glory of light which God gave you up within the shell of your physical body, and if any escapes at all it is too weak to stand up against the negative thoughts and incidents in your life which you are projecting on to the ether to your own undoing.

Light brings joy and joy brings glory, and when you have once held within your heart the glory of the Divine Consciousness all things are possible to you. It is not what you do in life that matters, but how you do it. Do you do it with a song of praise in your heart and realise that every action, from the simplest household task to the greatest volume of writings, is your gift to God. Have you prepared that gift for Him as He expects to receive it, or have you fallen away from the positive light of His Countenance and allowed the darkness of negative thought to dim the joy of giving?

When the Master Jesus was on earth men were living simple, unlettered lives. Mind and the development of the mind played very little part in their lives at all. The atom was

74

something which had never been thought of. Today the atom is a very real part of the material world, but it is still invisible to the scientists. It is only the occultist and the clairvoyant who can see the atom in the ether, and, as a rule, it is only the occultist and the clairvoyant who can assess its power. The whole of life, the whole of nature, is permeated with Divine Mind and that Mind is distributed to each and all, according to their own needs. Amongst a group of students there are not two who have the same needs, mentally, metaphysically, physically or spiritually. You do not draw the same vibration from the ether of light. You do not tap the power of Divine Mind at the same source. You are reaching out, and the great Spirit of Light touches you either on a low level of consciousness or on a high level of consciousness, but you do not touch it in exactly the same way as another.

The scientist can give you very deep understanding in scientific language of why two trees planted side by side, one an oak tree and the other a cedar tree, are different. They are both planted in the same soil in the same way. They are apparently drawing the same sustenance from the soil, and yet it is the Divine Consciousness of Spirit permeating the growth of those two distinctly different entities that gives you an oak tree and a cedar tree. You plant a rose bush and a blackberry bush and you feed them with the same fertiliser and you water them with the same water, but they are no more like each other than you are like your next-door neighbour, for the Divine Consciousness of Spirit differentiates between the blackberry and the rose bush in the same way as the Divine Consciousness of Spirit makes you different from the beasts.

The Gift of Intuition

Dual Mind is the linking in of the mind of man with the mind of God.

All life, all living things of nature, of creatures, are enfolded in Divine Mind, Divine Consciousness. Divine Consciousness is the discarnate Logos, the whole Mind of God. The creation of a planet is achieved when it becomes enfolded in the Mind of God; the God-consciousness pours through it, bringing it life.

You read the stories of the Israelites of thousands of years ago – the prophets Isaiah, Nehemiah, Job, and the chronicles of the Kings and the great deeds set down in the Book of Exodus, and you realise that these conditions of living were entirely different from the conditions which you, as incarnate man, are facing today. How are they different? In those days man was developed on the physical plane. He was entirely guided by the Mind of God, so that he could not alter his life, his movement, his being, because there was no mental development belonging to him or part of his life. The Divine Consciousness placed him where he was, guided him forward, and he obeyed that consciousness without question because he knew nothing else. In a sense, he was somewhat like a robot; he was set going by the Divine Consciousness of God, who kept him where he was and guided him on his path, and in a sense, it seemed as if man was much nearer to God in those days. It was not so much a question of nearness as a question of at-one-ment. Man was one with God and therefore he knew no other will or desire than the Will of God, but he had not developed on the mental plane.

Into that picture of apparent complete submission there came rebellion. There came men and women who no longer wished to be guided by God at all and He withdrew from the guidance until they had separated themselves from God and become a group of their own, functioning in matter and without intuition.

Here and there among the men and women whom you would call 'creatures' among those intermediate people there were those who had intuition, but the majority were entirely separated from it, and in being separated from it they were separated from the Love of God, which is the creative side of Divine Mind.

It was at that moment that it was ordained that Christ Jesus should come in order to teach these men to at-one themselves with God. They had moved away from Him; they found themselves in a state of turmoil and difficulty without knowing why they were in such a state. And it was Jesus, by His life and His teaching, who drew these men again into the orbit of the Logos, and by pouring into them the knowledge of the Love of God, helped them to reach out through material consciousness to the Divine Consciousness of Spirit. In this work, as you know, Jesus was helped first of all by twelve chosen Disciples and later His work was carried on by seventy disciples, and it is important to notice that only two or three of the chosen seventy were called to work beside Him; the majority were called to work in the world after His death and resurrection.

But it was Jesus who brought the full power of the subjective Mind of God into being in the minds of men and from that moment, little by little, the mind of man became a tangible and real thing and showed itself in its true light as the organ of the soul, the vessel within the soul which held the power of the Logos, the Creative Word, which became flesh through the Love of God.

It was particularly the Love of God that Jesus emphasises in all His teachings because He was dealing with a very material company of people who understood the objective mind, which is the mind of the materialist, whose organ is the brain only. What we must never forget is that it is only when the light of the soul pours strongly through the mind of man that the brain, which is the organ of the physical body, can be raised to the level of Divine Consciousness and used in the service of God.

You have watched, as the years go by, man developing enormously upon the mental plane. You realise that the mind of man is an incredibly wonderful mechanism today. It is a mechanism entirely of God. It is God-force, God-strength, God-power, God-light, and it is the intuitive centre of man's becoming. You meet in your daily life hundreds of men and women who appear to have no intuition. Many of them have a certain psychic awareness because they have a power of awareness of an objective nature through their objective mind, but that awareness will not reach further than the ordinary confines of the astral plane and therefore we must understand the right terminology to use. When we are using 'psychic' we are meaning 'astral' and when we say such a person is 'psychic' because he foresees material happenings and links in with material conditions a little in advance, or conditions which have already been completed, he is definitely reaching out through objective mind to the Subjective Mind of God and every step he takes in that direction brings him nearer to the Subjective Mind of God and nearer to the manifestation of his soul, which is the mirror of the Logos.

When a man seeks development on a higher plane of consciousness he becomes intuitive and through that intuition he is always looking for the causal point in life. He will realise that life is a cycle and that he is always coming back to the same point on that cycle, touching it from a slightly different angle. Therefore, he must find the reason for that constant return and he begins to look for the cause, the intuitive force begins to flow, and he sees the reason and accepts it as the way

79

of God. In those ancient days men were not aware of this God-force within them and around them; they appeared to be directed from point to point and life to life without any volition of their own. It was only when it came to the parting of the ways, the moment when the God-force given through the subjective mind was called upon to unfold also the objective mind of man in process of evolution that there seemed to be such a gulf fixed between God and man. In reality, the gulf exists far less than it did in the days of Isaiah; you are far more one with God than those ancient prophets; you have developed your mind, you have developed on the mental plane in such a way that the God-force flows through your subjective mind and merges your subjective mind with the subjective Mind of God.

You are travelling on the road of the individual. You are no longer one of a mass, a multitude; you accept direct from the Hand of God guidance, from the Voice of God intuition, and you yourself are a complete individual replica of God, because you have accepted from God the power of His own Divine Mind which you hold in your own subjective mind and endeavour to use through your objective mind towards all who move in material conditions as objective will only, so that the subjective mind, unfolding you and your consciousness, the opening out of your own consciousness to the knowledge which God is giving you, causes you to build up a channel for discarnate subjective minds who have gone a little further on the road than you have.

In the time of Isaiah the Israelite people moved in great masses, in large numbers, directed by this force, but that is no longer the case; man is an individual and the subjective mind of God is his. He is directed individually by that mind, and in combining the subjective mind of himself with the objective mind of himself, he is called upon to make a perfect whole, and through the lower mind to provide a channel for those higher forces of light which he has been able to accept from discarnate subjective minds who are called upon to guide mankind.

You find the subjective mind of God working throughout the whole universe. Where it meets gross matter, barriers are set up by the gross matter which prevent subjective mind penetrating. You cannot say or think even that the subjective Mind of God is able to penetrate the depth of great coal and iron mines. These are entirely enfolded in objective mind, but in the earth, in the soil, and certain places where the transmutation of objective mind into precious stones, a glory of beauty, which are not objective at all, which are so encompassed and transmuted by the power of the subjective Mind of God that they become mirrors of His Mind in the same way as you do. The fact that man has caused these beautiful mirrors of God to be used for his own purpose of power and financial advancement does not detract from their value, nor does it prevent them from shining with the full power of the Mind of God in those places where they are taken.

You will find the subjective Mind of God there because these are individuals. Coal, iron, clay, chalk, these are things which are masses, but the precious stones are individual mirrors of the Light of God and hold that light as the Mind of God itself holds its own Subjective Mind.

In nature we look also for the individual light. The Divine Consciousness of the Subjective Mind is penetrating very readily the world of nature. Never have so many differing blossoms and plants been discovered; never have men been called upon to work so much with the soil in the production of plant life, but for the complete and perfect example of the subjective Mind of God incarnate in plant-life you must go first to the lichens and the grasses. If you study these you will find no two heads of grass or blades of grass identically alike. If you take a bunch of lichen you will find it entirely different leaf by leaf in shape and form and if you plant that bunch of lichen in two different soils and in two different places you will find that its growth will be entirely individual in each place and entirely different.

But in nature the subjective Mind of God is manifest most

81

fully in the trees and it is the essence of the tree which holds the subjective mind. You will find no two trees with the same growth, the same shape, the same size. You will find these differences which mark them out as individuals in the world of nature.

It is the same with the animal kingdom. When a creature or a little animal detached from the group soul is brought into close contact with man, the more highly that man has been able to develop his subjective mind, the more he will be able to raise the objective mind of the creature to a higher level, until it becomes the mirror of the subjective Mind of God Himself.

The Pituitary and the Pineal Soul-Centres

There are certain negative and positive characteristics of the personal character which link with the soul centres and they are linked with the governing planet.

Man is spirit and God breathed into him the breath of life, and although we think of man as a being in the physical body, he is, in reality, spirit detached from the place of light to which he belongs, because he has promised to fulfil a service for his Father-Mother God which no other can fulfil. Therefore we find each individual man and woman and child entirely different from the other one. From time to time we come across two who are similar in features or two who are similar in character but we very rarely find two who are so entirely alike in features and in character; even in twins there are differences, and these differences depend upon the quality of the power of spirit which rests within the soul, and of that portion of spirit which the soul has earned in previous lives given to it to fulfil itself in this life.

Our soul centres or chakra are the focal points for light in the etheric body and they lie within the physical body, so that where the spiritual-psychic body penetrates the physical body, those centres will lie identically one upon the other in all the bodies.

But in many people these centres do not lie identically one

upon or within the other. We find that the centre of the spiritual body will lie a little outside the same centre in the physical body, or the astral body, or the soul body; it does not matter which body you consider, if the centre does not lie identically upon all the other centres there must be a disharmony or lack of rhythm. That disharmony may be quite a large force; it may, on the other hand, be nothing but a visible trickle, so small that it is no more important than the thread of cotton which you pass through the eye of your sewing needle. But even when it is as a thread, that thread can admit forces which do not belong to light and therefore cause disruption or disharmony, or the entry of a negative force through the aura of the incarnate soul.

The pituitary gland, or soul centre, is the most important of all these centres to spiritual man.

The pituitary gland links you directly with God. The light which you give from that gland may be dimmed by the time that it reaches our Father-Mother's vision. It can only be dimmed by your own mistakes and failures and difficulties, no one can dim the light from the pituitary centre for you; you alone, can dim the light yourself, and because that is the greatest spiritual centre of the soul-physical body, it is governed by Uranus, the great spiritual planet.

The colour of light given forth by Uranus is the colour of all light at its source, merged of many colours but entirely colourless, but by the time that light, or ray, reaches the aura of your spiritual body, it has become blue, and therefore it will be projected into your spiritual body and into your pituitary centre as a deep blue light. It is clear, although iridescent; it has an incredible power for calming and soothing; it brings with it all the gentleness of the love of the Father-Mother God, a love which is something not of the earth and which, in reality, can hardly be described in physical words; that tremendous force of love which creates round you the blue light of Uranus, passing through those infinite invisible planes between your Father-Mother God and yourself until it enfolds your pituitary soul centre, and your auric light is complete.

The healer uses this blue ray for soothing and calming his patient before treatment; he uses it again to fill the centre, the pituitary centre of his patient before he bids him farewell.

That vivid blue links you closely with the planet Uranus, and Uranus is responsible for sudden events, for sudden happenings, for great joys and great catastrophies; catastrophies happen if his ray is impeded or wrongly used, and when the ray is wrongly used we say it has been used on a negative vibration. So we see the pituitary soul centre enfolded in the light of Uranus, the distant spiritual planet of the Glory of God.

What are the character attributes of those whose pituitary gland is alive, and awake, and aware of this tremendous force from the planet? These attributes are two – they are positive and negative, and the positive attribute is humility; the negative attribute is pride.

The sin, or negative character attribute is pride; the virtue, or positive character attribute is humility. The centre through which the Grace of God is given for you to attain humility, the positive aspect, is the pituitary gland, or soul centre, and the power to help you to achieve that positive virtue of humility is Uranus.

The words, pride and humility, are hackneyed in your language, they have no longer the meaning that they had when they were first used to describe these aspects of the character of man. There is a chapter in one of St Paul's writings in which he speaks of charity suffering long and is kind, and charity has no more to do with the joy which is described in that writing than the kind of pride you remember when you think of earthly pride, has to do with the sin which is called one of the seven deadly sins by the early Christian Church.

Charity should mean love. Pride, rightly understood, means poise, completeness; it means a spiritual development of character where the soul guides the personality in perfect harmony, and the light pours through the pituitary gland, assisting your meditation, giving power for your concentration, from the highest source of spiritual light which man can touch – the planet Uranus. Those who possess this virtue in all its completeness go through the world of men without fear, they are evenly balanced, they are able to recognise truth and falsehood in the men and women with whom they make contact; they are able to see, through these men and women, the shallow empty lives behind them when there is no God; they are able, through that positive attribute of poise and balance, to move with surety about their daily tasks; they are able to hold the Word of God in their hearts because they draw upon that infinite source of light which never fails them through the pituitary gland.

That is true pride, which is humility, because humility, again, is a travesty of the great Christian virtue which was described by that word many thousand years ago. Pride of place, the knowledge that God is within you, the knowledge that you are able to walk through the world as a child of God, brings that humility of heart, which is proud enough or poised enough not to submit to the approach of darkness through man but always able to hold the power of light from God, which is the attribute of God.

But the negative attribute of pride, which you describe as pride in the world today, is perhaps known to you under different names – class consciousness, snobbishness – where you try to respect a man for his worldly achievements when they are purely the things of the world; the man who achieves greatness in the world because of his soul light you cannot describe by the negative force of pride. Pride is, to us, one of the ugliest sins that we can touch, for the great soul is humble, the great soul moves through life, poised and sure, complete in soul and body and spirit through the power which comes to him through the pituitary gland from the planet Uranus, the great servant of God's love.

Another important soul centre is the pineal gland; the pineal gland, which is represented as the old Third Eye, which sometimes closes the physical eyes of man that he may see with the eyes of the spirit, so that the man who is walking through life physically blind has a greater force in his pineal gland and would appear to be closer to the world of spirit than the man with physical vision. Through the pineal gland are given those impressions, those visions, those pictures, which man so often mistakes for something which comes from the higher planes of consciousness through the pituitary, the impressions and pictures which must never be ignored or neglected, for they hold the very Glory of God within them through their positive light.

The force of the pineal gland works with great rapidity and strength through that world which you call the world of imagination; the world of the writer and the poet through which they link to those higher worlds of inspiration and intuition, but they cannot touch the worlds of inspiration and intuition unless they are able to reach out on a positive vibration through the pituitary gland to the planet Uranus. The world of imagination lies very near the earth plane, it touches the soul as the wings of an angel brush the place of God. It is a quality which can be used with positive strength to portray truth at its very highest; it is a quality also which can be used in the most negative attitude of mind through untruth and falsehood and lying.

In dealing with the children of today we need to be very conscious of the force which flows through the pineal gland and to analyse whether it is true or false, whether the realm of imagination in which these children dwell is the realm of the spirit or the realm of the astral. If it is the realm of the spirit, then let us pray that we may add our own spiritual power to awaken the spirit within that world of imagination and strengthen the child through the God force which we can contribute.

The pineal gland is governed by the planet Neptune, and we all know what disaster the negative aspect of Neptune can bring, what weakness, what untruth, what ugliness of soul and personality, and yet what beauty, for Neptune is the planet of sound, and his ray brings sound rather than colour, and when we reach out to him we touch the harps of the place of light.

The positive virtue linking with the pineal gland, is meekness, and the negative virtue is anger. These are little words with perhaps very little meaning, but anger at its worst can wreck the world of imagination as nothing else can; the fire of anger is a consuming force of destruction, of destructive darkness, and it destroys all the soul quality which comes with meekness. Meekness, again, does not mean that you must forever turn the other cheek; it does not mean that you must humble yourself before the angry one and accept his dictum and be forced into his way of thought. Meekness again, because it is a positive force of God, gives you poise, the poise to know when darkness is unleashed, and you must defend yourself against it rather than do combat with it.

When anger is launched against you, remain firm and take no notice at all, even though it wounds you to the heart, just reject it. The quality, the positive quality which is poured through your pineal gland into your bodies of light is meekness, because it turns aside the arrows of darkness and leaves you radiant and full of light. You are called upon so often to show the positive quality of meekness, and in that quality your strength lies. It is not so much a question of turning the other cheek, as of standing for what is right within the sight of God and man, and then the force which is poured through the pineal gland lifts you above the crest of the wave of the world and leaves you with all the glory of the light of Neptune tuned into the sound of the spheres.

Anger which is launched in bitter words and recriminations moves upon waves of negative sound; meekness, which is still in the silence, is still in positive sound, so you draw to yourself direct from the great source of sound and inspiration the light of the planet Neptune who would guide you on your way to God. That guidance will come through the pineal gland, through the mind impressions which show you the character of your adversary, through the glory of light which overwhelms the giver to the fulfilment of light and life in those many planes which lie between you and the world of God, ringing with the music of the spheres.

So you have the pineal gland, or soul centre, under the influence of the planet Neptune controlling the negative force of anger and the positive force of meekness.

The Thyroid and the Heart
Soul-Centres

There are seven important soul centres of the body which function under various planets and control the conditions of the personality. We think of these seven soul centres as portions of our being which are called upon to pass through seven levels of purification. With a further five these form twelve, and we are called upon to undertake twelve tests. In fable and in fiction we know them as the Labours of Hercules, the Trials or Essays of the Knights of the Round Table, the perfecting of Discipleship in the world of men.

There is that wonderful centre, the throat, through which is produced sound, which can be pure to holiness and coarse to ugliness, according to the vibration upon which it is produced.

This soul centre, which is governed by the planet Mercury, contains within it the thyroid gland and that gland is a very important gland in the physical body. Through that gland sound is produced, through that gland thought is reproduced as the spoken word, joy is produced through laughter and happiness, anger is produced through the negative aspect of the gland itself.

The thyroid gland is one which is very closely linked with the nervous system and therefore when it is over-strained or the reserves of iodine upon which it depends for its sustenance are used up, the nervous system is considerably affected. With a deficiency of iodine the nerves can become taut and overstrung, they can cause irritability and anger and discomfort, but when the supply of iodine is sufficient to nourish the gland, no trial, no difficulty will ever appear too great to the subject because the nervous system will not be overstrained nor will a highly-strung condition manifest.

When we consider the planet Mercury, we realise how volatile and swift are the vibrations which must come in contact with the thyroid gland, the throat centre. We realise how much power Mercury draws from us, because the planets do draw power from men, do function upon the light and the glory which men can give out, and they function also upon the darkness and the negative attitude of mind which man can bring to bear upon his problems and upon his life.

The colour emitted by the thyroid gland is blue. When we look at the chakra functioning in perfect harmony in the throat of a highly developed student, we see a whirling wheel of irridescent blue light. The other colours are there but it is the blue which predominates and it is that blue also which controls the production of voice either in speech or in song and which draws from the ether notes and sound which it reproduces by way of the throat centre in the voice of man.

This throat centre can respond to spiritual vibrations on positive lines with an incredible strength. It can draw from the ether sustenance for man's being; it can create within the soul the glory of God. It is through the throat centre that Mercury, the invisible messenger works, carrying the voice, the tone of the voice, the texture of the voice, back to those planes of consciousness which lie below the Garden of Remembrance and within the Garden of Remembrance, linking you to those you love who have crossed the Bridge of Death before you, linking you by the power of your voice and the tone with those who guide you through the world of men from the spirit side of life.

Every word of joy, of pleasure, of positive strength, which is uttered creates a greater merging of light within which the thyroid gland can function. It produces upon the etheric vibrations of the astral planes a glory of light and colour, returning to the man himself, the subject, the words that he has used, the impressions that he has given, the glory he has set free, as a greater light in his benefit. That is the positive side.

The negative side is something of such incredible cruelty, such incredible darkness, that not only is the wheel itself slowed down, but the light which it emits is dimmed and dark. The positive mental attitude of mind creates anew light within the thyroid gland; the negative attitude of mind creates darkness of such density that it clogs the way of man in his journey on the earth. There is perhaps no gland or soul force within the body which can so rapidly create a darkness as the throat centre, especially in this coming age of Aquarius, for the throat centre is the centre of sound and sound is the glory of the Aquarian Age.

To the thyroid gland, because it is an organ of speech which you must use entirely in the physical world, you are linked with worldly attributes, and the one that is controlled by the negative aspect of the power is greediness – greediness for other men's goods, the desire to draw towards himself money and power in material things, the desire to hold within himself a greater place than his fellowman, to be marked and of note, and lose the simplicity which the Master Jesus called you to fulfil; greediness, which opens the doors to so many of the sins of the world, which causes man at all times to go against the law of man, whose origin is the Law of God; the greed for another man's land, the greed of one country for another, the greed of power in politics, the greed for power of place among your fellow men. All this is the negative attribute of Mercury, it is Mercury's influence upon the thyroid gland or throat centre.

Then, bearing that glory of the blue light in mind, we consider the beauty of the positive side of the throat centre, which gives you temperance in all things, the right balance, the right way of life, temperance which allows your wants and needs to be satisfied without too great a demand upon your worldly resources; temperance, which makes you contented with the place you are filling in the world; temperance, which shows you the light and the glory of the voice and the use of the voice and the sound which it produces.

This is the positive side of the throat centre under the planet Mercury, the Messenger, for the voice is the messenger from man to man of God, the words spoken are created things upon the ether, and when you speak your wish you create within the ether of light for good or for evil according to your way of thought and desire.

Then there is that vitally important centre, the heart. The heart, which is under the control of the planet Venus, which is represented by the positive aspect of brotherly love and by the negative aspect of envy. People in the world of men misunderstand the word love. They forget how the Master Jesus spent Himself to teach men discrimination, and to all those who are too swift to act, who demoralise others by their endeavour to carry the thought of love to a point which they were never intended to touch, demoralising men who perhaps have less strength of purpose, less initiative, than they themselves. Love, which draws men together, which shows both men and women alike the work which they have come to do in the name and in the service of God, which shows the creative power of love incarnate through the Trinity in the heart of man, and it is love that moves the bloodstream and the bloodstream moves through the heart.

The heart to the clairvoyant is a whirling wheel of rosy light, its core and centre like a deep crimson rose. The rhythm of the bodies of man lies in the heart. The seed atom in the heart contains the record of all your lives since you were created first of all from the power of the breath and the bloodstream within which flows the cosmic bloodstream, animates your heart and links you through the cosmic bloodstream to the stream of the life of God.

It is an important centre for it controls life and death; it controls joy and sorrow. It shows the purpose and the meaning of tears, tears which are the outlet of the emotions which come from the heart and which release from within the heart, pent-up emotions which should never have been repressed. As the planet Venus rises above you so that its vibration and light and colour are poured through into your heart all day long, your heart is warmed by the Venus light and by the linking with that great spiritual planet which lies behind the Sun, from which Venus draws her spiritual power to strengthen you through your heart centre in the physical world of men.

All the positive joy of friendship, of married love and the understanding that goes with it, love of children, love of friends and acquaintances, is dependent upon this great force which comes to your heart centres through the planet Venus.

On the other side of the medallion, because of the tremendous force of light which comes through that centre, because of the power of positive strength which it gives each one of you, the negative side must be equally strong, and terribly dangerous and difficult to overcome. Envy, which causes you to want what other men have, in such a way that sometimes you will sin to get it. Not so much, perhaps, as through the throat centre, for material gain, but for spiritual gain. Envy, which will make you want to take someone you care for away from a friend so that the friend shall not have his or her companionship. Envy, which will beat you down until your soul is in misery and error. Under the word envy there is so much resentment, that bitter sin which occurs so often from one brother to another brother who should have learned all there is to learn about the power of love and the way to get it, yet they will allow themselves to feel resentment against another. This can come through the spoken word also, and therefore there is a very strong link between the heart and the throat centre; for all the darkest sins of man can take away the glory of light within your heart.

What can envy do to the bloodstream? Greed can destroy your physical body through over-indulgence in food, through over-indulgence in miserly habits, holding to yourself what you have gained, but there is nothing that will hurt your soul so much as the darkness which comes in as the negative side of love; where the greater glory is, the greater darkness lies and very often, he who can reach the greatest heights of love can sink in a few moments to the greatest depths of calumny and malicious gossip, of envy and hatred and all unkind things. These darknesses beset you very much more when you become members of a group than they do when you are moving through the world without thinking of these things. Because when you join yourselves in brotherhood to one another you are setting the standard of God up in your midst and you must hold that standard high, you must hold it always from the positive angle, using your exercises of retrospection to make sure that during the day there has been no envy, no hatred, no malice in your thought or conversation. And if there has, before you sleep cleanse and purify your heart so that the heart centre may rise with light and create a greater light around you when you wake.

The Liver, Solar Plexus and the Sacral Soul-Centres

There are three further glands which are affected as soul centres by the positive and negative aspect of the souls under the guidance of the planets.

Jupiter is often created in the mind of man as a jovial God but, in reality, although he is on a positive vibration, full of joy, he has an exceptionally difficult task to fulfil with the souls under his guidance, for he must teach them to give; to give liberally to their fellowmen of their worldly goods, and their advice and their gifts, and to give with discrimination, which man incarnate in the flesh finds such a difficult lesson to learn.

So that the positive aspect of the gland is liberality, and as the soul forces of light press forward to enfold and surround that important organ of the body, the liver, which is also a gland as well as an organ, they have a tremendous task to do, for the liver is incredibly quickly affected by the wrong thoughts and actions of the personality. When it is separated from the soul, as man so often does separate his personality from his soul, the secretions which are held within the liver become dark and ugly and dangerous. In the covetous man the liver shrinks to a very small leather-like condition, and where you find in handicapped children a desire to grasp and hold on to everything they see, whether it is something which appeals to them or not, you are touching the negative aspect of covetousness through an organ which is small and congested and frequently lacking in right function as a channel for the light.

Healers should realise that when such an organ comes under a negative aspect, it not only darkens the secretions of the organ but it does shrivel the very substance of the organ itself, so that the liver will become cased in what looks – to clairvoyant eyes – like a skin preventing the passage of light through the etheric liver and becoming clogged and sometimes almost useless.

It is when covetousness, the negative aspect of Jupiter, manifests in the child and affects the liver that we find a condition of ill-temper arising, and that ill-temper can be conditioned considerably by emotions, which come under the planet Mars.

The colour of Jupiter, through all the bodies of man as his ray vibrates from the place of God towards the earth, is blue and that blue contains no light when you are observing the negative aspect of the light and vibration, but when it is on a positive vibration then the function of the liver is a radiating wheel of light and glory and fulfilment. The influence of Jupiter, on a positive vibration can be a thing of such beauty radiating from the outermost edge of the aura through the various bodies till it animates the great liver chakra and light is poured out through the chakra into the whole body of man.

Where you touch children who are inclined to be covetous, begin always by teaching them to give to others. They will give more readily to you than to their fellows, therefore keep on asking them to give, and give, and give again, until the desire to give is manifest in their gesture, in their eyes, in their actions and their voice, and once you have conquered that, you are clearing away the negative aspect and helping to adjust the action of the liver through the light poured into the chakra, the soul centre itself.

Another gland of great importance is the solar plexus, for that is the focal point of the astral rays, and at the solar plexus lies that vast network of the nervous system which activates the motor condition of the body. The chakra at the solar plexus is an immensely powerful wheel of light; it picks up the rhythm from the spinal centre and, moving in perfect balance, draws towards itself the rhythm and the light from all the other soul centres.

It is governed by the planet Saturn, and therefore when Saturn is in a bad aspect, conditions of the nervous system, stomach disorders, will be bound to occur because this chakra has such a vast influence on the very centre of the physical body of man. It can be easily clogged, and when it is clogged and becomes a negative attribute of the planet, it can cause considerable disturbances in the physical body; it can even separate the etheric bodies from the physical body, and very often the clairvoyant will see a rim of black round the body and close to the body, taking the shape of the body and appearing to cut off the auric light; this is because the negative attribute of the planet Saturn is in force within the solar plexus.

The positive aspect of the planet Saturn is diligence, activity, and you will realise that when you think that the gland, the soul centre, activates the motor muscles of the body. Under Saturn we think quickly, not with that mercurial quickness which so often leaves us without depth or understanding, but under Saturn we build diligently a sure foundation for the things of the spirit, and as the solar plexus centre moves round on its orbit of light it gives forth radiance and power for the mind and brain of man, to control not only his intellect and his intelligence but his whole bodily movements; it encourages him to be an active member of the community.

But when the negative aspect is in power then we find a very different picture, for the lazy, slothful people come under the negative aspect of Saturn, people who, oddly enough, will go to any length to avoid trouble to themselves or anything which can demand effort. You will find this negative aspect of Saturn in many of the backward children today because the positive side of them spends itself to avoid effort and occupation.

So the planet Saturn governs the soul centre of the solar plexus; on a positive vibration it represents diligence and activity, and on the negative vibration it represents sloth and laziness.

To understand the work which the Knights of King Arthur undertook and which we must undertake in our turn in the world of men, we study also the centre which is aspected under the planet Mars. The positive side of the centre is chastity in thought and word and action; the negative side is lust, and again lust in thought and word, in action, for has not the Master Jesus Himself said, as a man thinketh so is he. There is no centre of the soul manifest in the physical body of man to which those words apply with such positive strength as to the sacrum, or the sacral glands, which are aspected under the planet Mars.

Mars represents the warrior. The planet opposite Mars is Venus, and again there is no soul centre in the body where the balance is so important as under Mars. We must achieve perfect balance in the sacral glands if we are to be able to hold the soul within the body and manifest the soul as the light of God.

So we find Mars is the planet whose positive aspect represents chastity, whose negative aspect is lust, and who governs the sacral glands.

The most material purpose of the aspects, the most material action of the glands, and always the positive and the negative, must achieve balance, first under Mars, before the body itself can respond to the greater light which God gives to the soul. When the liver is activated by anger or distress, particularly by anger, Mars is very quick to know this condition and to shoot his lightnings into the soul organ affected, causing a burning up of the physical substance of the liver and a separation between the etheric auric light of the liver and the physical organ itself.

These seven negative aspects of the seven important planets in the life of man are represented in the halls of education and

100

reincarnation by the symbol of a red rose, and the work which most must undertake through initiation is to achieve the gift of the white rose through his experiences when he carries out the tests demanded of him under the red rose. The white rose is the symbol of intuition. The symbol of the red rose is initiation on the cross of matter.

When the soul leaves the Father-Mother God, a great preparation is made for his departure. If you could see the soul at that moment you would see a body of light, and that body of light enfolded and encompassed by other bodies of colour, still light but colour, and at the back the shape of the body – it is very difficult to describe these things in material words because the body at that moment is nothing but an ellipse, with the pineal gland at the top and the position of the feet at the bottom, and it is light. To that light is added the coloured rays necessary for the achievement of the purpose of incarnation; some of those rays will be stronger in power and colour than others, and behind the soul-body itself, which is surrounded with light, is placed a golden cross. That cross is also of light; it is the light of the spirit which will later be transmuted into the cosmic bloodstream within the physical bloodstream. The top of the cross is on a level with the head of the soul, the cross piece joins the upright at the place of the nerve centre at the top of your spine so that if you stretch your arms out they lie upon the arms of the golden cross and the upright continues to your feet.

For some time before you actually set out on your journey to earth, preparations are made for your departure and you will appear among other souls who are preparing for departure. Some of them will be ready to go with you, some will be going a little before you, others will not yet be ready, but you will mix and mingle with hundreds of other souls, some of whom will not incarnate again, others who will incarnate but have not yet begun their preparations or are probably not yet aware of the possibility. But you will be marked to them all as one who is going to incarnate into matter, because in a sense you are nailed to the cross, but the cross is a cross of light because that is God's gift to you as a symbol of Himself within you, the cross of light.

When you set out on your journey to earth, the cross goes with you. As you move down through plane after plane of consciousness, in each plane you touch less light and a greater density of ether. At the beginning that density will not be apparent but by the time you reach the Garden of Remembrance, which is the seventh plane of the astral sphere, your cross will become very much dimmed by the contact with the denser ethers which you are approaching, and at the moment of incarnation that cross will be absorbed by the seven centres we have been considering. It will be absorbed on a positive vibration or a negative one, and that depends entirely on yourself, for the absorption takes place at the moment of birth and if the soul hangs back at the moment of birth, the darkness is increased in the cross and therefore causes a great unbalance of these seven important centres, so that those of you who are working as healers and are conscious of reluctance on the part of your patient to face up to physical life to come to earth to be born into the material world, will find that the light is being projected in a very dark uneven fashion into those centres because of the negative attitude at the moment of birth which made the soul possibly even want to withdraw from incarnation altogether.

All the way from the Father-Mother God Himself that light is poured into your soul through the etheric glands we have discussed, and the soul alone can dim that light, the soul alone can accept the negative vibration in place of the positive one, for at the moment of birth every soul has the right to choose whether he will enter the physical world on a positive vibration or a negative one. It is at the moment of birth that the miser is born. He does not become a miser through life and through the action of life or the action of his parents or the way he is brought up – as a man thinketh so is he. And so often the miser comes to earth and at the last moment still holds the light of Jupiter to turn it into the darkness of negative thought at the moment of birth itself.

So that when we look at the glandular system of men we must consider the type of child, whether negative or positive at the moment of birth. We must further consider the child again between 10 and 12 months old, for at that moment the soul has a greater capacity for indrawing spiritual light than after the age of one year when the physical world is beginning to close in on it.

In your healing, treat the organs of the body which are aspected by the seven red roses, which give you the seven sins, if you wish, or the seven negative aspects of the planets which govern the soul centres of the body.

The colour of Mars is crimson; on a negative vibration it is a dead crimson rather like congested blood, but on a positive vibration it is shot through with the crimson gold of the lightning.

The colour of Saturn is green, a very soft and yet clear vivid green, not the green which we think of when we consider the Persian Healing Temple but much more an apple green, and clear so that you can see right through it.

The Etheric and the Astral Bodies

You have a higher mind and a lower mind. Both are within the soul; the higher mind links with God in the place of light, and the lower mind links with an astral condition which lies in the region of the subjective mind of the lower consciousness.

It is the great desire of all who seek to unfold the gifts of the spirit to reach into that higher consciousness where there is light, but between the lower mind and the higher mind there are a whole number of different strata which the student must master and understand before he can be ready to set aside the lower mind and embrace the higher.

The forces which work through the lower mind are prevalent to a very large extent in all forms of physical mediumship; that is common sense. They belong to the physical plane and although a psychic influence works through the physical medium, producing either fine or poor results it rests with that medium to raise the level of the plane on which he or she is working so that the light from the work can make contact with the light from the higher mind.

The light from the higher mind is much more static than the light from the lower mind; it is directed by the God-forces to the mind of all those who seek God.

But the moment that the higher mind begins to seek God the lower mind draws forces from the astral plane of a destructive nature which can be used to hurt and harm the light of the higher mind.

Again this is logical, for wherever light is produced, darkness, which is the opposite, must also manifest. The quality of that darkness depends upon the person who handles it. Are you reaching out to God and touching His light in such a way that if you enter a dark room His radiance is with you, or are you reaching out to the lower planes of consciousness so that you carry with you a darkness in your aura and etheric body which can harm the light which is produced by the higher mind?

The mind is the organ of the soul and the mind-body is enveloped in the etheric body, which is the exact counter-part of the physical body but really belongs to the soul. It is the vehicle through which the soul pours its light into the physical body.

The great centre of light in the physical body is the heart, and if the heart radiates light through love, compassion and truth and endeavour, that light radiates through the etheric body and forms that auric emanation of light which you speak of as the aura.

You will have seen that light round the head and shoulders and body of a man who is preaching from the pulpit, perhaps. If he is an ordinary man, seeking God in an ordinary way, that light will be a soft, very pale gold radiance, but very pale indeed, so that it looks almost lemon colour. If he is a highly-evolved spiritual soul that light will be of golden radiance of great glory and the depth of it round the head and shoulders will depend upon the degree of spiritual consciousness which the preacher has attained.

Covering all these bodies there is an astral body which is often misunderstood. It is of a much denser ether than the etheric body, and as the physical body throws off the emanations from the glandular system and the chakra into the etheric body these emanations are collected by the astral body so that the etheric body and the aura shall not be dimmed.

When death occurs the silver cord which is attached to the

heart is severed at the point of the etheric body. The etheric body carries the light of the heart and the soul over the bridge of death, so that if you were on the other side of life at the moment that a soul is passing you would see a dim light approaching as you stood on the edge of the astral world waiting for the crossing.

That light would seem to grow as it approached you. You would notice that it is in human form. What you are seeing is the etheric body enveloping the soul of the man or woman at the moment of passing. The silver cord broken, the bodies float forward smoothly and evenly, guided always by the light within the heart within the etheric body, and that light depends upon the spiritual strength of the soul, whose organ is the mind, which transmits the light given by God as a reward for service, through the etheric body, through the aura, that it may be a radiance to guide the soul towards the place of light.

Those words 'Man kindles a light in the night when he dies' are not imaginary; they are true, for the soul is at its greatest strength at the moment when it is going to leave the body. The way a man dies is entirely dependent on the condition of the soul and the link of that soul with God. We are not now talking of people who die from accidents or warfare or sudden death, but for the normal man or woman who dies in his bed that is the normal procedure.

It takes three days for the soul to compass that crossing and therefore the light that he carries will last him three days, when it dims and is replaced by the light of the spirit world which guides him to a place of rest where he will remain until the bodies are cleansed and purified of the things of the earth and he is ready to progress.

What about the astral body in all this? The astral body is of much denser ether. The clairvoyant can often see it like a chequered net, almost like a dark net curtain surrounding the physical body while the soul is still within it. It absorbs any darkness which can mar the progress of the soul, and taking the complete shape of the soul-personality, that is the person you have known on earth, it acts as a covering so that the change into the etheric worlds is not sudden or difficult. It has already absorbed the darkness which could mar the light of the etheric body and therefore it acts as a covering cloak and will remain until the soul is taken through the first, second and third planes of the astral and on to the Garden of Remembrance. When you die your friends wait for you under your tree in the Garden of Remembrance; they can only see you when you have shed the astral body and approach them in the etheric.

The astral body, being of very coarse etheric radiations, takes a very much longer time to disintegrate, and it moves about on the astral plane after it has left the etheric body it has protected like a dim grey shadow, the exact counterpart of the soul to which it was attached.

Slowly and steadily under the stress of vibration this astral shell dissolves, becoming fainter and fainter until it is invisible to the eye of the clairvoyant, but those who are studying psychic science must be very careful to distinguish between the etheric body of the soul that returns and manifests itself as evidence of life after death and the astral shell which is its exact counterpart, no soul is allowed to return near to the earth plane after it has passed unless there is some special urgent reason, when he is very carefully guided back. No soul is allowed to return until he has shed the astral body. He can only do that when his own soul is of strength and inner light to go on without the protection.

The astral body draws its life from the etheric body to which it belongs, and it can only dissolve very very slowly, for it is of the same composition as the ethers in which it lives and moves, and therefore those who have the vision must be very careful at all times to distinguish between the astral shell and the etheric counterpart of the friend or relative we want to welcome and describe.

The etheric body's radiance comes from the heart, but the astral shell has no radiance; it is a collection of astral particles, a certain amount of etheric light dimmed by the weight of the astral particles, so that it is very important to remember that the vision of the clairvoyant can sometimes be deceived by an astral shell, but those who are perceptive and intuitive or who are used as writing mediums can never be taken in by the astral counterpart.

As soon as the soul says to itself 'I want to find God; I want to reach out to a greater knowledge of the spirit world and the meaning of death', light is given for the progress which he shall later make, but at the moment the light is given, the objective mind comes into action and draws a great deal of darkness from the lower astral planes to try and hold back the soul from progressing in light.

It is at this moment when this happens that selfishness appears to be paramount. People who have never been selfish in their lives before become suddenly self-centred and selfish. We are not now thinking of those who are habitually self-centred or selfish but of those who are full of the desire to serve God with a knowledge of truth to which they adhere, knowledge of love which they manifest and prove. These are the children of light who will be attacked over and over again by darkness through the lower mind, and who will always hold sufficient light to be able to hold their own.

No man is tested beyond his capacity. Truth is light, love is light, grace and humility are light, and above all, strange as it may seem, gratitude is light, and it is the man who can give thanks gratefully, freely, truly, to his fellowmen and to God, who touches the higher consciousness of spirit and enters an open door.

But where we get one who is accustomed to falsehood, who is accustomed to self-seeking and self-centredness, those faults are doubled the moment that he seeks to unfold the consciousness; his untruth becomes greater and deeper, his self-centredness not only shuts out his fellows but closes the door on God Himself, and his lack of gratitude for all that is done for him by his fellows and by God, keep the door locked and barred against the light, so that when he thinks he is raising his consciousness to God he is drawing light from the place of light to hand to the darkness. That is why these faults open a door of such danger to all Sanctuaries and places of meditation. It is because untruth can attack truth and bar the door against truth in the raising of the consciousness and the seeking of God in the silence.

Many students are ready to meditate. They open with a prayer, choose a verse from the Psalms or some portion of the Bible or some other religious writing and they compose themselves peacefully and quietly, but so many forget to give thanks, and if you forget to give thanks you are forgetting one of the greatest attributes which links you to God.

It is a common practice today for parents to deny their children the need to say 'thank you' and they are wrong, doubly wrong, for the child who says 'thank you' glows within himself with the light of God.

And the student who kneels at the foot of the Cross and gives thanks to God is at all times surrounded with a radiance of light which lifts him without further effort to the higher consciousness of spirit.

You may put your hands in a bowl of warm water in Winter and mentally thank God for the blessing of warm water, and you may put them in cool water in Summer and thank God for the blessing of cold water; you raise your eyes in the morning through the window and thank God for a new day, and above all you walk under the trees in Springtime and thank God for the new life that is flowing throughout the world, through nature and into the hearts of men.

The child who says 'Thank God for a good dinner' is opening his heart to that very light although he is perhaps not conscious of it, and the child who learns to sit still during the prayer time or the singing of a hymn is opening his heart in exactly the same way, although he is not conscious of saying thank you for the blessing of silence.

I cannot emphasise too strongly the joy of the blessing of silence – silent gratitude which lifts its heart to God and which glows at every little word of praise and thanksgiving, at every opportunity to enlarge and strengthen God's work on earth, at every friend who comes forward to help to guide and to open a

110

new door of learning and wisdom – gratitude to the man who sweeps your streets. They are paid materially for their services these cleansers and workers in the material world; they are nevertheless fulfilling a service for which we owe very deep gratitude to God. It is God who manifests Himself in their work.

The great calamity of the world and particularly of this country at the moment is that there are so many hundreds of people overpaid for the service which they are giving, seeking, many of them at all times, to evade service and do the least possible thing that they can for what they earn or think they earn.

They spend as long as possible over a cup of tea and forget that every minute of that hour was paid for by someone. A sense of responsibility and of reverence can come back to the nation again if people such as you determine to hold the light, and to hold that light in the higher consciousness of spirit, putting up a barrier for the darkness which can come through the lower mind and destroy all the work of God.

The Will of the Soul and the Will of the Personality

The soul is an invisible part of man; it is the real man, the part of man which God created in His own image and directed to earth to become incarnate in a physical body through which he would accept physical life with all its joys and sorrows, its advantages and its disabilities, and endeavour through the power of the soul to regain the Kingdom of God by the power of light within him, and by manifesting that light, by enlarging that light and by creating beauty out of that inner light of himself.

The mind is an eternal thing. When the body dies the mind within the soul goes forward over the bridge of death animated by the spirit which is that part of God Himself which God gave to man to fulfil His likeness in his own body-personality during his life on the physical plane.

For this purpose man was given a physical body of a wondrous nature, whose mechanism is revealed as one of the great mysteries in the world and one of the world's greatest marvels.

The head of man contains the skull or is built upon the skull, and within the skull we find a strange mass of grey matter which under the microscope looks worth nothing at all and yet is responsible for the intelligence of physical man and for the guiding of his personality. That grey matter is the brain and the brain disintegrates with the death of the physical body, and some of those particles of dust which many years later will be discovered in the box in which the body is buried in the earth, will be part of the brain which has disintegrated into the dust and become part of the soil of the earth in which the man himself lived.

You can perhaps say that an ape has a personality; he certainly has a brain, a much smaller brain than man possesses, but nevertheless a brain which also disintegrates after death, but we must not forget that unlike the ape, the physical body and the brain of man are activated by the soul which is within man and the mind which governs the brain of man and through the brain of man sends the necessary messages for the control of the muscles and the cleansing and the purifying of the physical body and the bloodstream.

In the days when primitive man lived upon the earth one does not hear of him dying of disease. He lived to a great age, he lived a natural open air life and was not troubled much with his mind because he was very little conscious of his mind – in fact, the portion of mind which governed the personality of primitive man was a very small portion indeed, and it would seem on a casual examination, that only the brain of man manifested in the physical body of man even as it did in the ape. But this was not so because man was a living soul and our Father-Mother God had breathed into him the Breath of Himself which was the Spirit, and though he would seem to you uncouth and cruel and unusual, nevertheless the Breath of the Father-Mother God was breathed into him and that breath animated the spirit and the spirit animated the mind, and the mind poured its love and power through the brain and then through the physical body, governing its movements and its life.

But when our Father-Mother God created man and gave him a living soul He gave him one great attribute which is entirely absent in the members of the animal kingdom. The apes have it not, none of the great mammals have it, none of the creatures so far have it in the same way, and that is, that in

114

fulfilling the soul and body of man with the spirit of Himself and breathing into man the breath of His own life He gave man love and love linked man with God, and when God says 'I gave you life because I love you' and man says 'I give you service, O God, because I love you', he is expressing that great attribute of man which God gave to all men before they left His side to come into incarnation, and that was the Love of God, which is also the Will of God. For the Love of God creates in man the desire to serve God and the Love of God deflected from man to God and back to man again creates in God the desire to strengthen and increase that power of love. So through love the will of man was born and that will animating the soul, impregnated with the spirit of the Father-Mother God, that love becomes will, the will to serve; that love becomes God, the will to give.

So we see that the will is something which never stands still. As man desires with his love to serve God, God desires with His love to guide and direct man along the path, which in the nature of God is the path of love.

In the great days of Atlantis, man was tuned in to the Place of Light and his only desire was to manifest God in all His love in the temple, the place of the spirit, that the power of the spirit might go forth from the worshipping man to God and return as the great gift of love from God to man. Therefore the will of man was the Love of God made manifest, and so long as man was enclosed in the temple and only went abroad to cultivate the glories of the garden, he only used the will within himself, which God had created of love, to love and serve God, so that the will of man described a circle; it came from God and passed through man to return to God again.

All healers in the Temple of the Little Yellow Flower understood the power and process of the will, for the will was God's love. It was the submission of the will to the Love of God, the acceptance of the fact that God's love was greater than man's love in texture and quality and quantity, and therefore man was ready to place his hand in the hand of God and ask Him to lead him.

115

There are many stories, myths, legends – call them what you will, of the bringing of the first ugly side of the use of the will towards man, and that happened in the case of a great Chinese business man who had been healed in the Temple of the Little Yellow Flower, slowly and only by the love of God, which is God's will expressed in him in health, culture, success. He desired greatly to use the things of the Temple, which were the gifts of God, to make money and bring power to himself. From the moment that the question of power came into the picture there appeared within man a lower self, and the will was divided; no longer was the will of man turned entirely to the service of God; here was another service offering glory and power, fame and honour and position and many friends in the physical world which could not in any way be submitted to the will or the love of God.

So we see at that important moment the severance or the separation of the will of God from the will of man, and when we speak about man in this sense we are speaking of a man who has refused the guidance and therefore the love of God and has manifested within himself to the world of men an action of the will which now becomes entirely material.

The glorious roses whose perfume and oil had always been used for the healing in the Temple were dragged away and their precious oil distilled and sold for many hundreds of pounds. Was the money devoted to the building of temples? Was it devoted to the healing of the sick? No, it was used for the aggrandisement of man, to give man power and might and position and wealth and glory which he decided at that moment to spend on himself.

So we see the will of man, God, divided into two parts; the will of man God remained in the temple and the will of God withdrew from the will of man which manifested the self, the lowest possible form of self which man could manifest. The will became in two parts – one light and the other dark, and the dark part was the lower nature of man manifesting no longer under the direction of the will of God but apart from the will of God, taking a path of its own making, blind to its own development, blind to its own progress, and going forward drawing all things to itself.

If you talk to a man or a woman who is described as a schizophrenic you will find that there are some moments when they are entirely normal, when they probably have great charm of manner and personality and at those moments they are seeing the world and their fellowmen through the eyes of God, which is the will of God, which is the love of God. Then all of a sudden they realise that they are submitting themselves to God, and this won't do at all, and so they decide to hold their own in power and strength and love of their own selves, so that they themselves shall be dominant, wholly in themselves. And here was the first selfishness bred.

In talking to a schizophrenic the one thing that will strike you in the ugly lower mood is his selfishness, his self-centredness. You have a bag of sweets; he will not be content to share the sweets with you, he will want the whole bag. If you give time to helping him, talking to him and interesting yourself in him, he will want your whole interest, your whole time, and when he cannot get it he becomes angry, and why does he become angry? Because he has fallen from the love of God and is no longer directing his life under the guidance of the will of God.

Under the stress of modern life, that uncurbed, violent will which is so easily seen and described in the schizophrenic, is becoming a very important and ugly factor in the world of men. It is a sickness, it is a disease, and yet it is not a disease for which you can shut men up. It is only the severe cases, the really abnormal cases, which you can shut away from their fellowmen, and then they are so normally attuned to the will of God on the other side of the picture that there are times when you feel and know that they are quite right in a world of men who are endeavouring to think and act and work for their fellowmen under the guidance of God. That is where the great danger comes in, because the will of God can become at any moment, in such a person, cast out from the soul, and the soul will in insecurity, in great fear, in inferiority complex, call it

117

what you will, the soul will retreat into the nearest refuge, which is the unbridled will of the personality.

So we see that there is one will of the soul and that is the part of God. That will is the love of God made manifest in man. It is shown in man in unselfishness, in service, in the determination to sacrifice all for the regeneration of mankind and the betterment of an unhappy world.

Side by side with this there is this lower will altogether, where power and glory, and above all selfishness and self-centredness are the predominant factors. When you seek that side of your own personality-soul you are splitting the personality into two parts. The personality which manifests within the soul and submits to the will of God is the higher self, and that part of the personality which seeks only his own aggrandisement, his own power, his own wealth, his own joy, his own freedom, is the lower self. That lower self is now, through the stress of material life and also through the rising of the great water which must further engulf the world before Atlantis itself can rise from the depths of the ocean; that ugly lower self is becoming a dominant factor in the world, endeavouring to rule the heart of man, endeavouring to rule the world of man, causing greed and laziness and all the ugly immorality of your life today, to come to the surface and to show you the lower self of man in its ugliest and most unstable form.

There are cases in which not only is the lower will split away from the higher self, but the lower will is again split into two very unpleasant people, and the third is the higher self, the soul manifesting in light, accepting the will of God and endeavouring to follow its path.

You find these parallels in ancient history. There was a time when the temple priests held the whole power of the Court; the ruling of the kingdom was in the hands of the King-priest, the King-Queen priest if you wish, for they were twin souls. Then there came a moment when power and the desire for material power and gain and so forth, the desire for a physical crown came into being, and the lower self split away, and then you saw the Kingdom of Egypt separated from the Temple. The Kingdom of Egypt was in unbalance, because the Pharaoh of Egypt was the twin-soul incarnate and that kept the balance, but when the darkness of the lower self increased more and more and ugly things were done in the temple because the court demanded it, and uglier things were done in the temple, because the temple rather liked the ugly things advised by the court, then you find a totally different regime in the world, and you find the lower self predominating, the higher self invisible.

It is this period that you are going through now. You are seeing the darkness and the evil in the world of men. You are endeavouring to hold your own higher self above all this, to serve God with love, and through that love to unfold His will within yourself, so that it will no longer be His will which your will is obeying, but His will within you which is one with Him. You cannot do that if you allow your lower self to rise above it all. That is why it is so important that we have an understanding of the path of initiation, and that we should take that path with complete faith under the guidance of God, and although we must make use of the things of the material world, and make use of the lower self, we must refine and cleanse and purify that lower self until it becomes the will of God – God within.

The Cleansing Power of Spirit

When a mind is unbalanced it means that it is not linking up with the physical brain and in the same way, when a limb is broken it is unable to link with the other limbs in the body, and therefore in a sense if the mind and the brain are not completely in tune and in sympathy a certain portion of the brain falls out of use and can no longer be governed by the mind.

The mind is the organ of the soul-body; it does not disintegrate at death; it changes as the etheric body changes when it leaves the physical body to journey through the etheric planes to the place of light. If the work of that soul has been good the mind absorbs the light at the moment of death and that light is used to guide the soul through the various etheric planes to the place where it is called upon to rest, but if the brain is not used sufficiently in conjunction with the mind then the brain becomes sluggish and very often seriously diseased and in such a condition that the mind cannot use it, and the use which the mind puts upon the brain is through the development of the will; we have already noticed the importance of the development of the will, the will of the soul and the will of the personality being apart and yet together. It is the will of God that the will of the soul shall be in complete harmony with the will of the personality, but if the personality is endeavouring to follow its own wayward path the soul cannot control it and therefore the two fall apart and the will

121

of the personality, governed only by the personality, draws heavily on the grey substance of the brain without the necessary light which should be given by the soul being absorbed into its action.

The condition of the brain is considerably affected by the condition of the physical body. The mind remains always the same; the higher mind and the lower mind are linked together as the organ of the soul, and if the higher mind is stronger than the lower mind the power of the spirit can enter it and enfold it and guide the soul, but if the power of the lower mind is stronger than the power of the higher mind the lower mind sinks to the level of the personality and in a sense guides the personality, or misguides it, through life.

We are conscious that a very large number of the diseases which our medical men are endeavouring to cleanse and purify today are diseases which are entirely new to these highly trained specialists in medicine. They are groping and floundering in two separate channels. In the first, through their reluctance to admit an after-life and an etheric body, and in the second through touching physical conditions for which they have no known remedy and whose reaction upon the physical body they cannot explain.

When the great bomb was dropped at Hiroshima, very much more spread in the ether than was admitted to the knowledge of man, particles of immense strength and danger were released and these particles were absorbed by the ether itself. Some of these particles were much lighter than the air, others were heavier; those which were heavier came to earth much more quickly and resulted in attacks upon physical bodies a very short time after the release of the bomb itself. Others were very much finer particles and they were absorbed by the etheric itself, the etheric of the Earth, and many were held in the etheric of the Earth, moving round with the changes of the planets and the changing position of the zodiacal signs, sometimes coming very much nearer to the Earth, at other times moving further away. Where they remained long in the ether itself they affected the spiritual side of man's nature, particularly his spiritual vision, and they did not remain in that one spot in Japan – they travelled far, becoming part of the various ethers themselves. In some cases these, we can call them germs, entered the brain by way of the mouth of people who were already beginning to feel discontented with their way of life. They caused irritation in the etheric of the person or persons, they were discharged through the etheric of the person or persons into the physical body. In some cases they remained in the body, in other cases they were discharged, but in many cases they acted as a violent irritant between mind and brain, causing a minute channel between mind and brain and eventually causing the brain of the person whom they were attacking to seek such changes in his material life that the only thing he could see was warfare and the only thing he could smell was blood.

You will not find these germs only near the island where the bomb was exploded. They have travelled many miles, they have caused much disaster, and they are still very largely the inflammatory cause of man's dissatisfaction with life and his determination to see that his own personality is established, so that he forgets the way of God, the Light of God and the Power of God which rests within his mind and belongs to his soul.

These particles are constantly being released. Every time a Sputnik is launched into the ethers of light there is a certain amount of waste matter which falls to the Earth and that waste matter can be absorbed by souls who are suffering discontent and unhappiness. It can be absorbed by way of the mouth and by way of the etheric body. If absorbed by way of the mouth it enters the physical body and will attack any part of the physical body where any physical weakness lies; if it is absorbed by the etheric body it will be discharged into the brain and there will cause fret and irritation and discontent and severance of the personality from the mind and brain from the mind.

In order to combat these conditions you must just build your physical foundation to hold you close to the Earth. Only if your physical foundation is strong and clear and true can your spiritual foundation link you with the way of God, and that is why year by year we work always at the building of that material foundation. We have material jobs to do; we fulfil those jobs each day until we are weary, sometimes long after weariness has told us we should cease, and we fulfil those jobs because we believe that within ourselves is the very Light of God which calls us to unfold in His service the way of the spirit, and the way of the spirit is the way of the soul, and the way of the soul should be the way of the personality.

Have you within your soul one will guiding the personality in life, or have you two wills – the will of the soul and the will of the personality? If you have unfolded the will of the personality in material things for your own power and self-seeking you will most definitely find that the things of the spirit escape you, and then when you enter into the silence it is not the voice of God that speaks to you, but the voice of your own personality endeavouring to guide you away from the voice of God.

These material particles, ugly and dark, discharged from the missiles which are made for the power of man and the aggrandisement of man in the physical Earth are being discharged in large quantities into the ethers of space, and where these particles are heavier than the ether they are falling to the Earth, and where they are lighter than the ether they are being puffed and pushed about in the ether and kept away from man and mankind, but it is the heavy ones which are causing the physical diseases and these are diseases which are new to doctors and scientists alike, and a great deal of the work from the world of spirit is being spent now in entering hospitals and nursing homes where we can guide the doctors to a clearer and newer vision of what is happening to the bodies of man.

Modern doctors do not consider the feeding of man – physical man – any more than they consider it necessary to feed his soul, and unless the soul is fed with the light of the spirit and the body is fed with the right nourishment to make

124

bones and muscle and blood, the spirit and the body cannot possibly hold together. When your spirit is completely in control of your body the spirit is God; it is that part of God which God gave you to bring to Earth with you in an everlasting reminder that God is one with you and you are one with God. If the spirit cannot control the personality it cannot cleanse and purify the personality and the physical body of these particles of ugliness which will enter the body and cause disease. They are so minute, the Doctors are unaware of them; they enter sometimes through the etheric body and therefore through the chakra, and via the chakra into the glands, starting perhaps as a pain in the spleen or a discomfort in a kidney or in the liver or an irritation in the heart. They may settle in the lungs if your lung is not as strong as it should be; they will settle in other parts of your body and remain there, and because no part of the wonderful mechanism of the physical body which God has made can accept an intruder, for these particles are intruders, the organ of the body where that particle settles will endeavour to push it out and away, but unless the light of the spirit is strong and clear and full within the soul then that particle will remain in the physical body and will grow, gathering to itself darkness which will later be produced as the tumour and the cancerous growth, the duodenal abscess, and all the various ills which are new to us all because we are not looking for the cause in the right way.

You need to partake of the right food which will be absorbed by the bloodstream and the glandular system and the body itself, and no two people can partake of the same food and that food have the same result upon the body, because the preparation of that food within the mechanism of the body depends upon the power of the spirit which is within the soul. When we think of the power of the spirit within the soul we are conscious again of the organ of the soul which is the mind of man, and if man thinks rightly he will obtain a control over his physical body which nothing else can give him, and right thinking is thinking with God, not 'the way I want to tread in life', not 'the road I want to take', but 'the road which Thou has prepared for me to take'.

So in all preparations for mediumship our way is begun by a spiritual guide, a guide who never leaves us from birth to death. He stands back sometimes when the darkness is greatest, but who is always there and ready when we ourselves enlighten that darkness by the power of the light within our souls to come forward and join up with that great and glorious power with the things that matter in the invisible world.

It is the power of the spirit which will keep your body healthy and well. It is the power of the Love of God which will show you how much work both physical and spiritual your soul-body can undertake in the day, and it is that power of the spirit which will give you the power to fulfil the task which is yours to fulfil, and sometimes when you are breaking down over those tasks you are conscious of a determination to go on and finish them.

From time to time the physical body, animated as we believe by the greatness of a spiritual power which we can only feel in people, not see, breaks down under the strain. Why is that? Why does the physical body, guided and directed with such truth and exactness along the way of God, under the hand of God, under the guidance of God, by the power of His spirit, break down? Not because he undertakes too much of God's work, but because those who should be walking along the path beside him, to take part of the burden which he is taking fall away – they get lost in the fog of materialism and they forget their place is chosen for them and if they will develop their own spirit within them they must walk the way which they have planned with God and with those whom God has directed should lead them and walk with them, walk beside them. And what of these diseases of the great camps of Europe, the great internment camps which were broken up? Why has God guided the Jewish people to a country on their own? Why have so many heard the voice of God and obeyed it and gone back to Israel, why are there still so many who ought to be in Israel and have not yet gone there? Because in those

126

internment camps and those places of suffering they were continually subject to the attacks of germs of diseases which were known only in those camps, and they were germs which originated in the mental plane – they were the germs of intensity of suffering, and many of them are suffering in silence, and in silence the hideousness of these germs is greater than in the noise and tumult of life. So God guided those people who had given birth to children in those camps, who had worked in those camps, who had suffered in those camps, to one land where they would be together, and to that land He directed a great and mighty Ray of Power and Light, a ray which shall entirely destroy the germs of disease in those who are strong enough to be able to accept it. They must be physically strong; they must above all be spiritually strong, and because a Jewish man or woman is not a professed Christian, you must not think that the power of spirit passes him by. He came to Earth with the same power of spirit in such measure as he had earned it in previous lives. Has that Jewish man or has that Jewish woman developed and unfolded the power of spirit within him by obedience to God's law, then in his own way he has created the Spirit of God anew within him, and created that light which will destroy the germs of disease which hang round the etheric pattern of the place from which he came.

Further afield, in Africa, in India and many other countries, you are seeing these frightful results – starvation with internment and imprisonment. These are germs which are born of mental suffering, suffering such as most people have never touched or known, and for these people we ask your prayers. Pray that the light may enter their souls to cleanse and purify those souls of the terrible suffering which has left resentment and bitterness in their hearts.

These diseases of the internment camps can be carried – they can be carried to other places; they can attack weak bodies or weak minds of other men. Therefore we are endeavouring to guide these people who hold these germs within their bodies, who die under the attacks of these germs, to doctors who are spiritually able, under the guidance of nurses who are spiritually able, to listen to the voice of God in their work and so through their knowledge and through their acceptance of the guidance of God can come to a realisation of what these diseases mean and the way to cure them. They are attacking men on the mental plane as much, if not more than on the physical plane, and when the will of the personality is destroyed, by the will of the soul being separated from the will of the personality there is very little hope for the physical body of the man to whom these belong.

Preparations for the Age of Aquarius

During the present period we are working on an Aquarian ray and as we think of Aquarius we are conscious of a fresh flowing stream of light. This stream, when looked at as colour, is of a vivid blue. Where it touches the subject there are stray rays of aquamarine; therefore, the ray as it touches you individually is not entirely Aquarian.

The aquamarine ray links us with a certain period in Egypt. It has nothing at all to do with any planet or any zodiacal sign. It was a ray which was given specially for the working out of the Egyptian Cycle. Many souls in Egypt touched it and held it, other souls could not approach it, and that gives us the two great divisions in the reincarnated souls from the Egyptian era. The ones who could touch and hold the aquamarine ray, and could therefore bring that ray with them into this incarnation for the regeneration of mankind, and those who could touch the blue ray without the aquamarine.

We cannot go forward into Aquarius without realising the power and the value of that soft gentle aquamarine light. We are never permitted to visualise it, and therefore however much we sit and endeavour to hold it, to see it and to accept it, it eludes us. It is only when we have achieved the full power and glory of the Ray of Aquarius that we are able to distinguish the aquamarine light. For it is really a light, not a ray, and it is the key, or the clue to the opening of the door of Aquarius. The doors of Aquarius will be blocked by the wall; the doors in the wall will be firm and strong and locked, and they can only be opened by those who hold the aquamarine key.

This blue light may appear to us very much as the light of the Virgin Mother, and here we have yet another link, because we must realise that the work of Mary, the mother of Jesus, was not finished when she brought Him into the world. She brought the first stages of the message of Aquarius, and that message gave her the blue light which we always connect with the Virgin Mary. She probably was not conscious of touching Aquarius at all, and yet if we were to enquire into her life as a child we should be conscious of the large part the carrying of the water-pot and the pouring out of the water played in her life, thus giving a symbol to all who understood the symbolism of the Age to which her work and her life and her power was directed. She could not hold the blue Aquarian ray without passing it on to her Son, and that was one of the attributes which Christ Jesus possessed, apart and quite different from the attributes of His brothers and sisters. He was able at all times to accept the full power of the Aquarian Light as well as the full power of His life path, the Piscean Ray.

If you study the Gospel story you will realise how large a part was played in the life of Jesus by the water, and you will realise how that ray was passed on only to certain of His disciples, the two who passed the Beautiful Gate of the Temple and watched the rippling of the water pool. These were the two who were given, as a parting gift from their Master, the ability to touch and to hold the Aquarian Ray in all its fullness and its glory, and that was the Ray that they used in their healing work after their Master had left the Earth.

We must realise that the Aquarian Light, the Aquarian Ray, and all that concerns it, is of incredible purity, and you will find as you make more and more contact in connection with your physical, earthly work, that you are being brought in touch with many souls incarnated under Aquarius. They will be difficult to understand but that you will not mind, because you know that you have come to face certain difficulties and to clear those difficulties out of your path for yourself and for others.

These are the lower strata, the lower group of the reincarnated Aquarians. You will find that they have little spiritual power in the beginning, but get to know them better and you will realise the value of the soul. Although there are many hundreds of thousands in the market places where bargaining and almost sharp practise is carried on, you must learn to conquer the darkness that comes with these souls, for they are the foundation of the greater and more important incarnation of Aquarian souls to come.

We must all take the people of the market place first. We must meet them, we must learn to know them and to study them, to realise the reason that lies behind their actions and their words and, above all, not to expect too much from them. For here we are dealing with very simple souls who have come into incarnation for a material purpose alone; to build the material foundation upon which the next strata of Aquarian souls will come, much cleansed and purified by the work that has been done by the first group.

You must also remember that you are privileged to be born earlier, to live perhaps an even longer life than these souls. You are also privileged to meet many people of many types and you are given much help in your study and understanding of the psychology of the contacts you make. You may find you have an unrelieved and difficult task to fulfil. You may have been directed to work for, or with, one man or woman who shows the very difficulties that you have been taught to avoid in yourself. Try and realise that these souls are probably working upon the power of this first strata of Aquarianism, and therefore you must study them and understand them in the same way as Alfred Adler studied his child patients and their parents, always looking for the one point within the life of the soul which was worth touching, worth holding and worth building upon.

You will find that these methods are being used very largely by all who deal with delinquents, especially with the young delinquents, because in many of these early stages of incarnation the darkness of the Aquarian Ray is very much like the mud and the slime which can be found in sluggish water. It must be cleansed and cleared away, and if your laws are insufficient for it at the moment, you must endeavour to work and to pray for right guidance in all classes of the people, that the darkness may be brought to the surface and that those who hold this darkness may be shown the way of light.

Those who are strongly aspected under Capricorn have a very great and very grave responsibility because the Capricornian must climb, and wherever he places his foot, Saturn sharpens the rock on which he steps. The rock may look strong, it may feel steady and be steady, but if Saturn uses his tools upon it, it can cut and bruise and hurt. Therefore, we carefully examine our charts to see where Capricorn lies in connection with our own Sun sign, even if we are not actually born under Capricorn, so that we may know the work we have to do.

Hundreds of years ago many of us climbed that great mountain which led to the Temple of the Little Yellow Flower. Many of us worked within that Temple, laying the stones for the terraces and the paths, planting the trees and the herbs and the flowers, working as priests, as healers, as healer priests, passing through all the stages of the training which is necessary for the preparation of the healer priest, dwelling in complete isolation except for our brother workers on the top of this mountain, and yet we know that we could not have reached that height unless we had climbed. Some of us were taken up upon the backs of mules and donkeys, carried in baskets because we were too crippled, too insecure on our feet to make the climb ourselves. Some of us were healthy children whose parents had heard the call for service in the great Temple and who handed us over to the man who came down the mountainside with the donkey and the baskets, knowing that our life was to become dedicated to God. But by far the larger number of us climbed that mountain on foot, and long before we reached the top our shoes were worn through and we were left to face the bitterness of the sharp rocky pathway with bare feet. If we arrived in the Temple exhausted we were left alone to recover.

That is very like the life which Capricorn ordains at this day of time as a preparation for the life under Aquarius. All those who are going forward to work with Aquarius must climb the great mountain, must find the path, and difficult it will seem as the path will be rocky and stony and sharp. And only when we have accepted ourselves as having achieved a height, as having set aside the difficulty, having faced the point of no return with courage, will the healer be allowed to come forward and give us nourishment and take us to a hospital where we can recover, not from the darkness of man, or the deadening life of the world but from our own inner self. That was the meaning of the mountain of Capricorn.

It is very much the same now, for those who are born with a strong aspect to Capricorn must cleanse themselves and others and the temples of the karma of the past. We must accept that. We must realise that being born in this particular Age means that we not only accept our own karmic disabilities for cleansing but the disabilities in which we share in the temples of darkness, for there may be no darkness under the light of Aquarius. Only when all the mud and the silt and the filth have been cleared away will the clear waters of Aquarius be given to us to allay our weary bodies and to soften the weary souls.

The Sagittarian has much to cleanse and purify in this life, for he has reached the point when he must prepare to accept the cleansing of the sign of Capricorn, and he must learn the meaning of not only accepting his own karmic difficulties but the difficulties of the temple and those who served with him in the temple. He must learn to withdraw his arrows, to break

133

them into three pieces and to fold them away, but to keep the bow as a symbol, for without the arrow the bow can bring nothing but light and strength and power.

Therefore, if the Sagittarian finds that he is using more of his arrows than he should do, let him learn day by day, week by week, and month by month, to break the arrow into three parts and accept the symbol of the bow. For that is the symbol that we are given when we make contact with a soul born under Sagittarius. Is the arrow set in the bow, ready to spring, or is there no visible sign of the arrow, only the exquisite light and glory of the bow?

The Sagittarian has further to go than the Capricornian, as he climbs the mountain to the Temple. The Capricornian sometimes is inclined to stop on the way to listen to the sad story, or a complaint, or to look at something which pleases his fancy. This he must not do, for every one of these incidents means a delay and while the Capricornian is climbing the mountain on the one side, the Aquarian power is waiting for him at the top. Therefore, if the Capricornian is late, the waters of Aquarius will be withdrawn until another time.

The path of the Capricornian is not an easy one. No one who has a strong aspect to Capricorn in his chart will ever be able to evade his difficulties. He may be held back by friends on the side of the path, he may be held back by his own desire to give and to help those who are in sorrow and in trouble, but he must be absolutely firm, remembering that not only the progress of his own soul depends upon his firmness of attitude and his determination to hold the light, but also the souls of many who study him, who oppose him, who agree with him, and who walk beside him.

Your horoscope, rightly drawn, shows you the pattern into which you have been born; the opportunities given to you and the situations you must meet. It is for you to tune the will of the personality to the will of the soul which is guided by God, that you may fulfil the obligations laid on you from the past and take advantage of the opportunities afforded to you.

One day, man will know that what he achieves in the sleep

state is not only as important as that which he fulfils in the course of the day, but the one is inseparable from the other. What he prepares in the sleep state he can pick up intuitively the next day and, in working it out, prepare for the work of the next night.

If he attunes his will to the will of God when he sleeps, he creates the pattern for his next days work.

Thus he walks in harmony in his own etheric pattern. The sacred vessel, his soul, will be filled by the waters of Aquarius to hold the light of the will of God.